THE FORMATION OF THE IRISH ECONOMY

The Formation of the Irish Economy

EDITED BY

L. M. CULLEN

THE MERCIER PRESS

4 BRIDGE STREET, CORK

First broadcast 1968
Radio Telefís Eireann (Radio)
© Contributors 1969

ISBN 0 85342 051 3

Reprinted 1976

THE THOMAS DAVIS LECTURES

This book originated as a series of Thomas Davis lectures broadcast between January and March 1968.

Every autumn, winter and spring since September 1953, Radio Telefís Éireann has broadcast half-hour lectures, named in honour of Thomas Davis (1814-45). Inspired by one of his sayings, 'Educate that you may be free', the aim of these lectures is to make available in popular form the best work in progress over a wide field of Irish scholarship.

Many of the lectures have been in series, many have been single broadcasts. Most have been in English, some in Irish. They have dealt mainly with Irish history, literature, society, geography and economy. Most of the lecturers have been Irish but many have been scholars from other countries. A considerable number of the lectures have been published, either in book form or as articles in periodicals. There is a list of all the Thomas Davis lectures to April 1967, with particulars of their publication, by Rev. F. X. Martin, in *Irish Historical Studies*, no. 59 (March 1967).

CONTENTS

I

THE IRISH ECONOMY IN THE EIGHTEENTH CENTURY

· BY

L. M. Cullen

The condition of the Irish economy in the eighteenth century has often been misunderstood. Depression was not prevalent, as historians have suggested. Moreover, to the extent that depression prevailed in the early decades, it was a consequence of low prices and poor markets abroad, not of British policy. After the 1720's recovery was strong, and it was expressed in industry no less than in agriculture. The policies of Grattan's Parliament were not responsible for the economic growth of the closing decades of the century. Indeed, during those decades, a growing contrast between social classes emphasises that its policies were powerless to deal with tendencies that were to prevail in the nineteenth century. The contrast between this interpretation and that traditionally accepted lies in the misleading nature of contemporary writings.

In the study of economic and social history we necessarily rely to a large extent on the writings of contemporaries. Yet excellent though these sources are, they often fail to throw light on the wider aspects of economic and social life. The writers after all, understandably, took for granted on the part of their audience a familiarity with the background to the events about which they wrote. But hundreds of years later, it is the economic and social background more than the ephemeral events through which we glimpse it that fascinates the historian. In practice our limited and inadequate knowledge of social and economic life is often based on contemporary sources not intended as a serious assessment of these conditions at all. In such circumstances, it is easy for the modern student of the past to draw misleading conclusions.

An example may illustrate the point. The well-known poem *Cúirt an Mheáin-oidhche* or *The Midnight Court* by Brian Merriman is a satire about male reluctance to marry in eighteenth-century rural Ireland, a topic indeed with a familiar ring to modern ears. As a satire it is hardly a primary historical source, but the historian could, and has, used it to illustrate a point. The picture of rural Ireland emerging from a study of Merriman's poem, limited through it necessarily is, could be regarded as according with the established view of chronic poverty in rural Ireland. 'Farms are bankrupt', we read in the poem, and elsewhere in the same poem we read 'that Ireland's fortunes still decline, that all our rights are swept away, that our cattle die and our crops decay'. But it is misleading to see in such statements confirmation of the accepted picture of rural Ireland. The poet wrote in 1780. In that year the country was only recovering from severe depression caused by bad markets and tight credit in these islands in 1778. It is in such conditions that one expects to find bankruptcies and to encounter complaints often embroidered with exaggeration from farmers. As far as long-term trends are concerned, bankruptcies suggest former substance, and the relevance of Merriman's poem, if it is of any interest to the historian, is that it suggests a picture different from that which we have come to accept of peasants who married early and who had little economic substance.

There is, of course, a great mass of contemporary writings. Some of these writings profess to discuss economic issues often at some length. But their interest in economic matters usually had its origins in concern with economic difficulties arising either from poor markets abroad or bad harvests at home. Bad harvests feature disproportionately in contemporary literature. Better harvests in the intervening years were often taken for granted. Writers were all the more prone to exaggerate the persistence of economic difficulties because, offended on constitutional grounds by several measures of the English parliament binding Ireland in economic matters, they were anxious to prove that their economic ill-consequences were as pervasive as their constitutional implications were repugnant. The case most in point was the woollen act of 1699. Little was made, at the time the act was passed, of its economic consequences. But almost a generation later, in 1720, the celebrated *Sixth of George the First* affirmed the constitutional dependence of the Irish parliament on the British parliament. This measure led contemporaries in their indignation to attribute the economic difficulties experienced in the 1720's to the act of 1699. It was now confidently asserted that there had been an emigration of thousands of Irish woollen weavers to the continent. No such emigration had, in fact, taken place. Low farm prices were also attributed to the effects on the economy at large of the loss of a foreign market for woollen manufactures consequent on the act of 1699. Low prices were, however, in no way a result of the act. This was a period of prolonged agricultural depression. Ireland's circumstances were not exceptional.

But if not exceptional, they were none the less serious, because Ireland as an agricultural country lost through worsening relative prices in the exchange of agricultural products for imported manufactures and luxuries. Prices of beef had already, of course, for long been depressed. This has usually been attributed to the exclusion of Irish cattle from England in the 1660's. But even for beef, the root cause of low prices was a surplus of beef in relation to demand. This had itself been responsible for the exclusion of Irish cattle from England; it was responsible also for the limited alternative outlets elsewhere. However, satisfactory prices for butter and wool had gone a long way towards sustaining the Irish agricultural economy. But butter prices collapsed at the end of the century, and agricultural prices generally a few years later. Given these circumstances, farmers could look forward to high prices only when disaster in the form of bad harvests or epidemic animal diseases either reduced domestic supplies or, as in much of the second decade of the eighteenth century, enlarged foreign outlets. The 1720's was the most difficult decade of all. Even the expansion of the linen industry appeared to be threatened with depression occurring early in the decade and again at its close.

The writings of Jonathan Swift, the dean of St. Patrick's, reflect the economic difficulties and the political resentment, both acute in this decade. The economic and political problems were distinct issues. Their origins were also diverse. But in polemical constitutional writing it was only natural to strengthen the case by confusing both. Swift's *Proposal for the universal use of Irish manufactures* appeared in 1720, provoked by the *Sixth of George the First*. Under a title of apparent economic significance, it was a political tract, and was instantly recognised as such. His savagely ironical *Modest Proposal* appeared following the famine of 1728-29. To contemporaries this famine was all the more alarming because it was the culmination of several years of poor harvests. They mistakenly thought that the shortage of grain was more the consequence of an abandonment of tillage in favour of grazing than of fortuitous factors. Their alarm was all the greater because the shortages seemed a prelude to even greater ones in the future. However, in the intervening years harvests were bountiful and plenty brought low prices in its train. The farmer had as much reason to fear plenty as scarcity. It was the close succession of a bad and a bumper harvest that was most likely to reduce the rural community to misery and indebtedness.

Economic conditions improved after the 1720's. The change was due to three factors. The first was improvement in the relative prices of cattle, evident already in the 1720's and leading to a definite though limited substitution of cattle grazing for tillage. For contemporaries, haunted by the fear of famine, the trend boded ill. In reality by making it possible for farmers to reduce their dependence on commodities in which prices were often very low, the trend helped farmers to maintain or improve their incomes on balance. The second factor was the growth of the linen industry. Duty-free entry to the British market in time made possible the substitution of Irish linen for much of Britain's large imports of German linen. However, in the 1720's, the future prospects of the industry appeared to be dimmed by the reoccurrence of depression twice within the decade. In every subsequent decade, however, except the 1770's, the industry expanded rapidly. The effects were most apparent in Ulster, but the spread of weaving and especially of yarn spinning into Leinster and Connaught brought some of the benefits of the industry's growth to families far outside the main centres of weaving in Antrim, Armagh and Down. Thirdly, harvest failures were fewer, or where they occurred, the shortfall in supplies of grain was, except in 1740-41, made good by massive imports. It was, indeed, in part the large grain imports that filled contemporaries with foreboding. The temporary tightening of credit that such large imports led to, added to their alarm.

Better though subsequent conditions proved, either domestic harvest failure or bad foreign markets for Irish products could still have a strong adverse effect on the economy. In particular, harvest failure worsened the plight of rural labourers and town dwellers alike by high prices and scarcity.

For the farmer himself, the benefits were few because the surplus for sale was small, and imports, of course, served to limit the rise in prices. As for the linen industry, its growth added to dependence on foreign conditions. Depressed linen markets reduced weavers to poverty. If bad harvests and poor markets for linen coincided, distress in linen weaving districts was especially serious. This was the case in the worst years of the 'twenties, 'forties, 'fifties, 'sixties and early 'seventies. The emigration of weavers to America was less a continuous feature of life in northern Ireland than an intermittent trend in which the number of emigrant weavers, a mere trickle in the expansive periods, soared in the distress years.

Famine or severe food shortage was far from being an uncommon feature throughout Europe. The years of famine in Ireland in the first sixty years of the century, 1728-29 and 1740-41, and of acute dearth, 1709 and 1757-58, had their parallels elsewhere in Europe. It was, in fact, precisely the simultaneous failure of harvests elsewhere as well that prevented the rise in Irish imports, though sharp, from being commensurate with needs. On the other hand, if harvest failure in Ireland was not accompanied by failure in other markets, the rise in imports proved sufficient to prevent famine. This was the case following the disastrous harvest of 1744.

The population of the country was more or less stable in the first half of the century. It was only from around 1750 that a definite rise in numbers became perceptible. The explanation for the rise is a complex one. The potato may have played a decisive role. But it seems certain that less extensive harvest failure or in years of failure more abundant imports of themselves reduced mortality. If this is the case, one might regard the potato's role as purely subsidiary in promoting population growth. But one thing is certain, whether one regards an acre-economising crop such as the potato as cause or effect of population growth, and that is, that as population continued to grow in the late eighteenth and early nineteenth centuries, the proportion of the population relying on a potato diet increased.

Generalisation about the condition of rural-dwellers is difficult, however, with reference to incomes, diet or other circumstances. A common mistake has been to assume a homogeneous Irish peasant with no security of tenure and no capital resources of his own. The occupiers of the bulk of the land were tenant farmers protected by long leases of 21 or 31 years, or for lives. The length of the leases itself contributed to the difficulties of tenants in periods such as the early eighteenth century or the 1770's because, though prices fell, tenants' contractual obligations did not diminish. On the other hand, when prices rose, as they did throughout the greater part of the second half of the century, the rigidity of long leases was very much to the tenant's benefit. It was this circumstance and not a clearly defined tenant right that explained why a tenant selling his interest in a lease with a number of years to run could realise a substantial sum from the incoming occupier. Catholic tenants, as opposed to Catholic middlemen, did not suffer from the restriction, before 1778, of their leases to 31 years. The landlords, aware of the drawbacks of long leases, were beginning to adopt a policy of commonly granting shorter leases to Catholic and Protestant tenant alike. This policy, along with a growing aversion by landlords to middlemen who were the main beneficiaries of very long leases, had the effect also of under-mining the middlemen. In any event middlemen, the extent of whose acres and influence has been greatly exaggerated, had been entrenched only in the poorer regions. The irrelevance of middlemen to the fundamental issues affecting rural Ire-land in the eighteenth century is seen in the fact that the impoverishment of rural Ireland in the half century before the Great Famine proceeded despite the rapid decay of the middleman system, even in its former strongholds.

If we can say with some confidence that the tenant farmer's condition has been too darkly painted, we can have no such confidence in looking at the condition of the labourer after the middle of the century. Labourers were themselves far from constituting a homogeneous class. Some were housed by their farmer employers; others discharged the rent of a plot in labour to a tenant master. For both, if wages were low, security was at least an asset. Others were less secure: they rented plots for a cash rent, and sought wage-paid employment as it was available, in some districts through seasonal migration. These workers benefited by rising wage rates and greater opportunities of employment in the rapid development of market production which took place between the 1750's and 1770's. However, it is clear that labourers and cottiers had not everywhere improved their lot in this period. Even Arthur Young admitted that their condition had worsened in some regions. In the following decades their condition deteriorated over a wider area, and except where spinning occupied members of the family, distress was often acute. The rent of land continued to rise; money wages had often ceased to advance despite rising prices. Where wages were not supplemented by other income, conditions were often as bad as in parts of Munster, where according to Fitz-Gibbon in 1787 'the lower order of the people are in a state of oppression, abject poverty, sloth, dirt and misery not to be equalled in any other part of the world'. FitzGibbon exaggerated only in suggesting that poverty of this degree was confined to Ireland.

The rural community below the level of landlord or middleman was thus far from being the homogeneous one often suggested. Dietary differences were striking between tenant and cottier; the potato diet appeared first among cottiers and labourers, and never came to dominate the diet of farmers in any part of Ireland. Again, the tenant farmer did well from rising prices. The cottier or labourer, on the other hand, often had to pay a competitive rent for his plot without in many instances the compensation of higher money wages or more regular employment. The conflict of interest between tenant farmer and cottier was thus a sharp one. Low agricultural prices might well bankrupt the farmer, but for the labourer or cottier they meant either cheap food or a lower value set by the farmer on the agricultural land a labourer might seek to rent. High prices made the farmer prosperous, but for the labourer they led to dear food or to a growing reluctance on the part of the farmer to part with a small plot of agricultural land at all. In areas where commercial farming was not well-developed, access to land was not difficult. Occupiers were prepared to subdivide their holdings, and the leasing of lands in partnership often facilitated this. But where commercial farming was well developed, the farmer was reluctant to grant plots beyond his own labour needs, and even then often in the less convenient locations. Young noted as he passed through County Limerick that 'land is so valuable that all along as I came from Bruff, their cabbins are generally in the road ditch; and numbers of them without the least garden; the potatoe land being assigned to them upon the farm where it suits the master best'. As population grew, a contrast emerged in time between poorer areas where every one had access to land, and richer lands where a much more commercialised farming prevented the fragmentation of farm land. In the poor districts what was striking even to contemporaries was the equality of everyone. A correspondent of the London *Times* in 1845, for instance, described Menlough, Co. Galway as 'an overgrown democracy. No man is better or richer than his neighbour in it'. In the richer parts of Leinster, Munster and Connaught, however, the contrast between relatively prosperous farmers and under-paid and intermittently employed labourers and cottiers was becoming more pronounced. It was in some of most fertile parts of Ireland, not in the poorer lands, that agrarian unrest made its lasting appearance.

It may seem surprising to refer to Ireland as an industrial country in the eighteenth century. Yet an industrial country Ireland was in the sense that industrial handicrafts were widespread in rural areas, and in the towns there was an important and growing industrial base. Skills in weaving and spinning were the most important. Domestic occupation in textiles proved essential to the maintenance of rural income as population grew and sub-division of land took place. In the north it was the poorly commercialised nature of agriculture rather than the reverse that facilitated the growing specialisation in the linen industry. But the importance of all this rural activity should not lead us to overlook the expansion of factory industry. It is widely assumed that such industry was not only limited, but declined in importance until a short-lived recovery was made possible while Grattan's Parliament lasted. The first eighty years of the century are generally regarded as a period of depression. There was, in fact, no long-term depression. Periods of depression for industry were short-lived, occurring when bad markets abroad or poor harvests at home led to tight credit within the country. Banking did not add to instability, because banks and their customers alike were at the mercy of external trade conditions and domestic weather. Firms were of course on a small scale, but this was typical of the age. It was only in industries such as brewing and glass where Irish firms were slow to adjust to changes of scale taking place in England that firms succumbed to outside competition. But by the 1770's larger firms were appearing in imitation of English practice. Industrial recovery was under way in these industries, and

Grattan's Parliament came into being only in 1782 after the decisive industrial changes had already taken place in Ireland.

We find ourselves in face of a situation in which reality is a good deal different from what is often asserted. First of all, the condition of the economy and of economic society was not as dark as the accepted interpretation suggests. Not all peasants were oppressed and down-trodden. Historians have all too readily assumed a homogeneous peasant, marrying in poverty at a remarkably early age. There is little evidence to prove an almost universal shift to earlier marriages in rural Ireland, or to justify the assumption that prior to the Great Famine of 1845 conditions were everywhere akin to those that had emerged in the areas officially classed late in the nineteenth century as the congested districts. If we turn aside from the rural scene to industrial development, we see that there was no chronic long-term depression, and that the century was marked by industrial resilience. Secondly, it is doubtful if official policies or legislation expressing them, friendly or hostile, at all greatly influenced the evolution of the economy. As far as English policy is concerned, measures affecting external markets for Irish products or the supply of some raw materials were of political rather than economic significance. In Ireland itself, interest in these measures was intermittent, and it was political unrest, marked in the 1720's and 1770's, that was decisive in securing acceptance for some sweeping generalisations about their effects. Within Ireland the economic policies of Grattan's Parliament did not create the economic expansion of the late eighteenth century. The decisive factors were the imitation before 1782 of new organisational features or, as in cotton, the exploitation of new technological possibilities. In any event, far from being a period of unqualified prosperity, the last two decades of the century were marked by accentuation of the contrast between tenant farmers and the rapidly growing cottier population.

It is indeed precisely in these two decades that generalisation about rural conditions begins to become dangerously misleading.

Irish economic development in the eighteenth century has a paradox about it. The observer must explain how the apparent rise in prosperity turned readily in the nineteenth century into the tragedy of famine and economic decline. Two factors are highly relevant to a satisfactory explanation. The first was population growth. This was not confined to Ireland. Population grew as fast or even faster in some other countries. The second was the Industrial Revolution. At first the influence of the Industrial Revolution was on balance helpful to Irish economic development. Improved technology or new forms of organisation actually restored the fortunes of ailing industries such as brewing and glass and made possible the expansion of the cotton industry. But in the long run the Industrial Revolution led to striking reductions in transport costs, the localisation of industry in favoured locations and the replacement of narrow markets by wider ones. What promised well for Irish industry initially, held out different prospects in the long run. Industrial decline in the nineteenth century was itself but part of a process of impoverishment in industrial terms at any rate affecting much of rural England as well. Taken in conjunction with population growth, this development had especially serious implications. They were foreshadowed before the Great Famine by growing underemployment among domestic workers. The fact that as late as 1841, 700,000 persons in a population of eight and a quarter million returned their occupation as being within textiles, is an indication of how important and pervasive a supplement to rural incomes from agriculture such employment had become. It suggests also how its decline would imperil the fortunes of the growing number for whom income from land or agricultural employment was inadequate or intermittent. Some historians would add a third factor, the slump in agricultural prices after 1815. This, however, affected rural areas throughout Europe, and of itself it could hardly account for the changes which took place in Ireland. In a sense it was not because Ireland was a non-industrial country but because she was an industrial country that she had so much to lose in the great economic transformation which affected all countries in one way or another but Ireland perhaps more than most.

II

THE RISE OF THE LINEN INDUSTRY

BY

W. H. Crawford

The rise of the linen industry in the north of Ireland in the eighteenth century had a profound effect on the subsequent history of this country. Because the industry established itself there the north developed differently from the rest of Ireland and evolved an individual and characteristic society. Historians have attributed this development to the peculiar advantages which Ulster enjoyed over the other provinces as a result of her colonial origins. Some have regarded government aid for the linen industry as an acknowledgement of Ulster's key role in the Protestant ascendancy. Others have held that the prevalence of the custom of Ulster Tenant Right protected tenants, encouraged them to make improvements to their holdings, and enabled them to create reserves of capital. There is an element of truth in these judgments but an analysis of the economic development of Ireland in the late seventeenth and eighteenth centuries will show that they were largely irrelevant. The questions which really have to be answered are: — Why did the linen industry establish itself in the north in the late seventeenth century? Why did it fail in the south? And finally, what effect had the rise of the industry on the economy of the north and on the structure of its society?

The English government made several attempts in the seventeenth century to promote the linen industry in Ireland. Laws were passed to encourage the growth of flax and linen manufactories were established with skilled workers from France and Holland. Lord Deputy Wentworth's scheme in the 1630's came to nothing. When the Duke of Ormonde ceased to be Lord Lieutenant in 1669 his employee, Colonel Richard Lawrence, noted that his projects soon failed but he made an important exception of Ulster where 'there is not a greater quantity of linen produced in like circuit in Europe'. This prosperity was due, he said, to 'the Scotch and Irish in that province [who] addicting themselves to spinning of linen yarn, attained to vast quantities of that commodity, which they transported to their great profit, the conveniency of which drew thither multitudes of linen weavers.'

British tradesmen had been attracted to these northern counties in the aftermath of the Cromwellian wars. Although the country was very poor it promised a good living for those who wanted to make a fresh start and were prepared to work hard. Landlords needed tenants to rebuild the estates which had collapsed during the 1641 rebellion after a mere thirty years of existence. Consequently they were prepared to grant good leases at low rents. Money was scarce, commodities were very cheap, and the cost of living low. The post-war recovery was very slow and was hindered by bad harvests and lack of capital. In such a poor and disturbed economy enterprise came from individuals who needed to succeed in order to survive. Such were the skilled tradesmen who hazarded their future by immigrating to Ulster from northern England. Many of those who came to farm also engaged in the industry and sold the linen cloth they produced in their slack time on the farm. As a result the industry was not confined to the towns at this vital stage but spread throughout the countryside, especially in counties Down and Armagh.

Many English settlers established themselves in the Lagan Valley and north Armagh. Puritans came to escape the persecution which followed the restoration of King Charles II in 1660. Prominent among them were the Quakers who established meetings throughout the area. Their records provide a valid sample of the immigrants for some of them were converted to Quakerism after their arrival in Ireland: almost all of them had been tradesmen in the north of England. The value of the Quaker community to the development of the industry in Lurgan, county Armagh, is great as their descendants were among the foremost linen drapers of the town and the advances they made in the industry were of national, not merely local, importance. The success of the industry in Lurgan during these initial stages was due also to the local landlord who gave active encouragement to his tenants and established a linen market in the town by buying up all the webs of linen that were brought to it.

Three miles away in Waringstown, county Down, Samuel Waring established a colony of Flemish weavers in the early 1690's. Better known is the enterprise of Louis Crommelin who set up a French colony in Lisburn, in 1698. Crommelin was probably 'the Frenchman well skilled in the manufacture' who had been sent in the previous year by another Frenchman, the Earl of Galway, to reconnoitre the country so that he could advise the government about legislation for the linen industry. At any rate Crommelin and his followers were given government encouragement and subsidies to settle in the Lagan Valley. This Huguenot colony was gradually absorbed into Irish society but their arrival was important for it boosted morale in the industry and the French techniques were copied by local weavers and bleachers. By 1704 the linen industry in the north of Ireland was flourishing so that a Bristol merchant wrote: 'the people in the north of Ireland make good cloth, sell it at reasonable rates, and would every year make much more, had they a vent (market) for it; and it is to be observed that money is not plentier, nor rents paid better, in any part of Ireland than there.'

The linen industry was on the verge of a new period of expansion. The chief stimulus was provided by an act of 1696 which permitted plain Irish linens to enter England duty free. This concession was to give them a great advantage over continental rivals in the English market. Ireland obtained immediate benefit from this act as the wars between England and Louis XIV of France shut out regular supplies of linen from Holland and Saxony. England became the great market for Irish linens and as late as 1773 she took ninety per cent of the total Irish export.

Historians have tended to regard the encouragement of the linen industry by the English government merely as a sop thrown by England to Irish pride while depriving her of the valuable woollen industry. They assumed that the woollen industry would have been able to compete successfully in European markets with the much more efficient and highly organised English industry: yet in Ireland the commercially successful branch of the industry was, on the admission of a contemporary, confined to the corporate towns where its expansion would have been limited by the restrictions of the guilds. It should be recognised, too, that government encouragement for the linen industry was not a new policy: for the previous forty years successive English governments had been recommending successive viceroys in Ireland to encourage the linen industry in addition to the fisheries and the provision trade. There is no doubt, however, that the fierce national pride aroused by the English government's policy towards the Irish woollen industry did benefit the linen industry. No longer was the linen trade a 'poor abject trade' in which it was impossible for 'men of a free generous spirit to engage'. Instead it now secured the patronage of parliament and in a spirit of patriotic ardour was born the Board of Trustees for the Linen and Hempen Manufactures. Those Irish who saw the woollen industry claimed as the staple industry of England were determined to make a success of the new Irish staple industry.

The Board of Trustees, established in 1711, was composed of seventy-two of the most eminent men in the kingdom including at its creation the law lords and many noblemen as well as the archbishops of Dublin and Tuam. Its task was to regulate the industry, to subsidise worthwhile projects, and to spread the knowledge of methods and techniques throughout the country. In its early days the Board did valuable work. In the first twenty-five years of its existence it paid out £150,000 of government money and on the model of the great woollen market at Blackwell Hall in London, it provided in 1728 a White Linen Hall in Dublin for the sale of bleached linens. The creation of the White Linen Hall put the industry in touch with Dublin merchants who were able to provide both the capital essential for the expansion of the industry and facilities for exporting its products. Indeed, the linen drapers found the Board valuable in these early years. But later as the drapers gained experience in the trade and secured contacts with English merchants on their own account, they began increasingly to regard the Board simply as a source of finance, as an intermediary with parliament, or as a stick to keep order among the weavers. When it was strong enough to control them, they resented its rather conservative and condescending attitudes. After they successfully defied it in 1782, they despised it.

Without the active encouragement of the Board, however, serious efforts would not have been made to establish the industry outside the province of Ulster. While spinning was widespread in the southern half of the country, weaving spread only slowly into parts of Sligo and Mayo and into the eastern counties of Louth and Meath. To speed up the process the Linen Board was, therefore, inclined by 1740 to foster the industry in the southern counties by establishing manufactories which would conduct all the stages in the manufacture of linen from the preparation of the flax to the production of the finished cloth. There was nothing new in such a proposal: it was the traditional method of sponsoring the introduction of an industry in any country at that time and had, in fact, been attempted several times in Ireland within the previous hundred years. The Board was no doubt reassured by the initial success of the De Joncourt cambric enterprise founded in Dundalk in 1736. Similar undertakings were executed throughout Ireland of which the best known are those of the Smith family in Waterford, Thomas Adderley at Innishannon in county Cork and Sir Richard Cox at Dunmanway in county Cork.

Before long, however, it was clear to the more acute observers that this method of encouraging the manufacture throughout the kingdom would never succeed. Although these projects were not difficult to establish they did require heavy and sustained injections of capital if they were to survive. Frequent bankruptcies of Dublin calenderers who finished their cloths and acted as their agents, adversely affected the prospects of the provincial manufacturers. It was easy also for the manufacturer to price himself out of the market either by concentrating on the finer linens in order to get some return on the capital invested, or by purchasing yarn when the price was too high: this could happen if there was a shortage of flax in bad seasons or if there was a heavy English demand for yarn. An even more serious limitation was the lack of skilled weavers prepared to work in these manufactories. Altough there were many thousands of weavers in the south they preferred either to weave woollen cloth or if they were linen weavers, to concentrate on the traditional but commercially worthless narrow cloths, known as 'bandle linens'. Consequently manufacturers were often compelled to import skilled weavers and bleachers from the north with the inducement of good conditions and wages. They were all too often placed at the mercy of combinations of workmen demanding more wages and the collapse of many schemes was attributed to this factor.

About 1760, Robert Stephenson, one of the shrewdest observers in the industry, warned the Linen Board that the manufactories in the south were not economically viable. He put forward an alternative scheme to subsidise public markets in the southern provincial towns for brown (unbleached) linens so that they would develop on the pattern then common in Ulster. Since there already were many weavers, it was proposed that they should be encouraged to weave whichever kinds of foreign cloth most resembled their own original products. The Linen Board adopted this idea enthusiastically and agreed to grant premiums for the public markets. The nobility and gentry of many of the southern counties entered into the scheme with enthusiasm for they saw how the linen industry had swelled the incomes of northern landlords. The premiums provided by the Board and the country gentry were designed not only to encourage weavers to weave cloth fit for export but also to subsidise drapers to purchase the webs produced, bleach them, and sell them in Dublin.

This scheme was perfectly feasible and in its early years it successfully surmounted several hurdles. The inexperienced southern drapers found that they had not only to compete with the experienced northern drapers but also to overcome local vested interests: the Cork and Limerick linen drapers who sold northern linens locally did not wish to see home-produced linen undercut their prices, and yarn jobbers who made large profits from exporting yarn to England did not wish to see it woven locally. The Board's schemes needed time to take effect. About 1770, however, there were complaints that the Linen Board was failing to pay its premiums:

this effectively damped the enthusiasm of the nobility and gentry who withdrew their subscriptions. Although this was a blow to the morale of the southern drapers and weavers they were able to weather it.

In 1773, however, the industry in the south was among the first victims of the serious depression which affected the whole of the British Isles. It was reckoned in county Galway in 1773 that 814 out of 1,000 looms were idle; in county Longford 800 looms were idle from Ballymahon to Longford and Edgeworthstown; around Athlone and Kilbeggan in Westmeath the trade declined by two-thirds and around Clara in Offaly by one-half. Many weavers abandoned their looms for good and one southern witness reported to parliament that many of them had emigrated. The enthusiasm shown by both weavers and drapers only a few years previously, evaporated and although the industry did survive, notably in county Cork, it was never considerable again.

The depression of 1773 seriously affected the industry in the north also: two-thirds of all the looms in Lurgan and Belfast were idle as well as half the looms in Lisburn and one-third in Coleraine. Yet, in spite of this serious setback with its consequent emigration of skilled workers to America, the north recovered because there the industry was more securely established. The economic structure of the north had evolved to suit the industry and the land system had become subservient to it. Where the industry was carried on most intensively a large number of individual weavers and small manufacturers supplemented their earnings in the industry by labouring tiny farms. They had found from experience that in this way they could secure themselves best against the fluctuations of the price of oatmeal, 'the bread of the north', and retain a certain degree of independence from the linen drapers. Towards the fringe of this area the industry was carried on mainly by farmers and cottiers and their wives who wove in their spare time to augment their incomes from the land. The depression therefore caused most suffering among those weavers who had forsaken agriculture and depended for their living on spinning and weaving.

The subdivision of estates in Ulster into small parcels to provide small farms for linen weavers, had been the subject of complaints to the Dublin Society as early as 1737. The practice was condemned by improvers. It meant that the land was not being valued according to its worth for farming but that an artificial value was being created based on earnings from the linen trade. Attempts were therefore made by several landowners to settle weavers in towns or villages by building cottages for them but they failed because weavers appreciated the value of their small farms even if they were prepared to pay higher rents for holdings convenient to the market towns. As weavers were able to pay higher rents than farmers, the process of subdivision continued on an increasing scale throughout the century so that by 1800 in county Armagh, for example, the average size of the farms was only five acres.

The success of the industry was therefore a key factor in the great increase of population which Ulster experienced in the eighteenth century. It helps to explain why the most densely populated county in Ireland in 1841 was Armagh (511 persons to the square mile) while the neighbouring counties of Down, Tyrone, Monaghan and Cavan, all linen counties in the eighteenth century, had more than 400 to the square mile. As the population grew, the dependence of the weavers in the main centres of the industry on purchased foodstuffs grew. Many thousands of people in the Lough Neagh basin owed their lives during famine in 1745 to imports of oatmeal through the recently opened Newry Canal while a contemporary referred to 'the second relief of Derry' when ships brought oatmeal to save the starving inhabitants of the Foyle Valley. Before the end of the century it was noted that 'in many parts of the great manufacturing counties of Ulster, the people are so numerous as not to be able to procure milk for their families, or flax ground, and depend almost entirely on markets for their oatmeal and other provisions;' The income from the industry provided a livelihood for very large numbers so that landowners were prepared to supply spinning wheels or looms to needy tenants in order to enable them to become self-sufficient and to pay their rents.

The demands of Ulster for provisions stimulated agriculture in the neighbouring counties. McParlan wrote in his 'Statistical Survey of the County of Sligo' in 1802 that Sligo together with Mayo was the principal granary and potato support of the manufacturing counties of the north in times of scarcity, and that the quantities of potatoes, oats, and barley produced there were immense. Over twenty years earlier, in 1780, another observer had noted that a large proportion of the bills of exchange remitted to absent landlords by their agents were drawn by Ulstermen in payment of sheep, horses, and black cattle purchased in Connaught and Munster.

In Ulster itself the success of linen caused a decline in the standard of farming. Arthur Young was right in blaming the linen industry for the failure of northern farmers to adopt modern methods of agriculture. They could not plead ignorance of them since many of their landlords were improving their demesnes and home farms in this way. Yet even if the industry had been confined to the towns as many improvers urged, it is doubtful whether a class of substantial yeomanry and freeholders would have arisen in the countryside with the capital to make such agricultural improvements. Only in counties Antrim and Londonderry did such a class of substantial farmers appear and even they were dependent on cheap labour by cottier sub-tenants who, in their turn, were dependent on weaving to make a living.

Relations between landlord and tenant in Ulster improved throughout the eighteenth century due to the economic prosperity generated by the linen industry. Ever-rising rent rolls made landlords less eager to enforce restrictive clauses in leases and more ready to commute them for money rents. Penal clauses against the alienation of leases were less readily invoked when the incoming tenant was likely to be solvent and legal proceedings were slow and expensive. The commonest kind of lease became the 'lease for three lives' which was extended to Catholics after the repeal of the Penal Laws, and tenants were rarely denied the privilege of renewing their leases if they were prepared to pay the current value of the land. We should therefore seek the explanation of civil disturbances in the late eighteenth century not so much in antagonism between landlord and tenant as in periods of depression in the linen trade or in pressure of population.

What were the sources of the capital which enabled this industry to expand so rapidly in the eighteenth century? It is obvious that the capital needed for spinning and weaving was very small and that substantial amounts of capital were required only in the bleaching and finishing trades. A small number of Quaker inventories of wills which have survived suggest that in the initial stages Quaker linen drapers drew on the savings of small farmers. Some capital too was borrowed on mortgages from merchants in Dublin and Belfast and some from landowners. Later, English merchants interested in the Irish linen industry provided capital. As the century wore on the returns from investment in the industry must have proved considerably greater than the return from land. Examples of public investment which benefited the industry were the construction of a fine road network based on the turnpike roads and the county roads, and the cutting of the

Newry and Lagan canals.

The eighteenth century saw no radical improvement in weaving techniques because the flying shuttle was not widely adopted until the nineteenth century, but there were substantial improvements both in the preparation of flax and especially in the bleaching and finishing trades. The early bleachers were quick to adopt Dutch techniques propagated by skilled observers the Linen Board had sent to Holland, and they obtained from the Linen Board substantial help in the construction of bleach yards. By the middle of the century they were highly competitive in the English market. As they came increasingly to depend for their supplies of potash for bleaching, on imports from the Baltic, Spain, or North America, the location of the industry was limited by the cost of transporting potash from the ports and the cost of carrying linens to Dublin. These factors tended to centralise the industry still further and confine it to north-east Ulster. The Londonderry region, for example, annually exported great quantities of yarn directly to Manchester because the merchants found it was more profitable than to make linen cloth for sale in Dublin. It was to save the cost of carriage to Dublin that the northern linen drapers in 1782 decided to build White Linen Halls in Belfast and Newry, a move which ended Dublin's influence on the development of the industry.

The year 1782 heralded the rise of Belfast to challenge Dublin's role as the clearing-house for Irish linens. In that year the northern drapers rid themselves of the last remnants of the Linen Board's authority over them. The Board continued to function until 1828 but the real leadership of the industry had long before passed to the northern drapers and bleachers. The Board had never played a decisive role in the rise of the linen industry and its failure to enforce regulations on weavers, bleachers and dealers proved to be to the benefit of the trade. The very remarkable expansion of the Irish linen industry in the eighteenth century was due to the great demand for cloth in England, to Ireland's privileged status in the English market, to the growth of an economy in Ulster where agriculture was subservient to the industry and, in the last resort, to the enterprise of Irish merchants.

III

CATHOLICS IN ECONOMIC LIFE

Maureen Wall

The penal laws passed against Irish Catholics after the treaty of Limerick affected their economic activities in a number of ways. In particular, they had the effect of channelling Catholic enterprise into industry and commerce to a greater extent than might otherwise have been the case. By these laws Catholics were prevented from buying and inheriting land in the usual way, and between 1691 and 1775 it was estimated that the acreage of land owned by them fell from 22 to 5 per cent. They were shut out completely from the professions of the law, the army and the navy, as well as from all positions in central and local government. For catholics of ambition and initiative there remained a choice between emigrating or remaining at home to make the best of the limited openings available to them. Well-to-do families found places for younger sons as officers in the Irish Brigade or in other continental armies. Some Irish Catholics set up in business abroad, especially in France, Spain and the West Indies. This type of emigration, however, was limited in scope and provided few or no opportunities whereby a man of little or no means could hope to improve his fortunes. A common soldier might earn his keep in the armies of Europe, but he was unlikely to be in a position to help his people at home either by remitting money to them or by bringing out his relatives to a better life in his adopted country. Emigration to the British colonies in North America was possible, but Irish Catholics did not emigrate there in any considerable numbers until the second half or indeed the last quarter of the eighteenth century.[1] Catholicism would have been almost as much a liability in the material sense in America as it was in Ireland, and the tradition of emigration for Catholics was towards Britain and Europe rather than towards the New World.

What were the openings available to them at home in the eighteenth century? As far as land occupancy was concerned they could take leases for not more than 31 years. A clause that the rent should not be less than two thirds of the yearly value seems in practice to have been unenforceable. Otherwise the substantial investment by Catholics in livestock in grazing and dairying would hardly have taken place. Grazing or dairying could provide only a limited number of openings for investment, and many enterprising and ambitious Catholics were forced to seek their opportunities in trade, an area of life which had to a great extent escaped the network of the popery laws.

They were, of course, for obvious reasons shut out completely from one occupation – that of making or selling arms or ammunition. They were also forbidden by law to have more than two apprentices under pain of a fine of £100 for each offence, and a hundred pounds was a considerable sum of money at the beginning of the eighteenth century. It is, however, difficult to state with certainty how far this limit on apprenticeship operated to the serious disadvantage of Catholics. I have not seen it mentioned in any contemporary

[1] After 1763 when England acquired Canada, and Catholics there were granted very generous terms, Irish Catholic leaders sometimes spoke of mass emigration to Canada as a solution for their problems. The threat of large-scale emigration by wealthy Catholics, unless they were granted some measure of relief, was frequently mentioned as a grave danger to the country's economy by members of parliament and others who were active in forwarding the Catholic relief bill which became law in 1778.

list of Catholic grievances and it was probably to a great extent disregarded. According to *Sleator's Public Gazetteer* for 28 December 1765, Protestant printers in Dublin were complaining that Catholic printers, in spite of the laws, were employing as many as four or even six or seven apprentices, not only in Dublin but in Cork and other parts of Ireland as well. Most business concerns in the country in the first three quarters of the century were run on quite a small scale, and there was no law to prevent Catholics from employing as many unskilled workers as they pleased, or persons who had already completed their apprenticeship. Moreover the limitation on apprentices did not apply to the linen manufacture, which was the country's main manufacturing industry, and the statute which prohibited Catholics, under pain of severe penalties, from sending their children under the age of twenty-one years abroad, without licence from the government, specifically exempted merchants' apprentices. The law debarring Catholics from leasing property for more than thirty-one years was probably one of the chief obstacles placed in the way of Catholic traders and manufacturers.[2]

---

[2] If a Catholic took a lease for longer than 31 years or at a rent less than the law allowed, a Protestant discoverer could deprive him of his interest in the property. A writer who has examined this problem in some detail estimated the number of discoveries under all headings (and there were many grounds for discovery apart from the two under discussion) for the whole country between 1716 and 1779 at 970 cases. Of these 67 took place in Dublin city. (See John Meagher, 'Of the genus called discoverer' in *Reportorium Novum* i. pp. 443-60). There was a steep rise in discoveries from 1750 on, which is probably explained by two factors.

One is that about this time the right of Catholics to lend money to judgment debtors (i.e. to lend money on the security of the borrower's estate under an agreement whereby the lender could receive profits from the estate, though he could never enter into possession of it) began to be questioned in law, and this made such agreements discoverable. The other is that most discoveries seem to

With a leasehold interest of merely thirty-one years, few Catholics would be encouraged to extend their business premises or to invest much capital in other than moveable property.

The sections of the popery acts of 1704 and 1709, which aimed at restricting within very narrow limits the ownership of property by Catholics, were directed mainly against owners of estates and took little cognizance of Catholics engaged in commercial pursuits. As a result the number of these increased rather than diminished and by 1718 we find Archbishop King of Dublin writing: 'I may further observe that the Papists being made incapable to purchase lands, have turned themselves to trade, and already have engrossed almost all the trade of the kingdom'. This statement was alarmist. It would certainly not have been true of the city of Dublin, where Protestants throughout the whole eighteenth century and for long afterwards, controlled the great bulk of the trade, nor of Belfast or Derry where few or no Catholics of substance were to be found. In Cork, Limerick, Waterford and Galway, however, and in many of the towns outside Ulster, they consolidated and extended their trade during the

have resulted from family disagreements, which were bound to increase with the second and third generation. Many discoveries were filed with the connivance of the defendant in the case, the discoverer holding the title in trust for the defendant, but whether the discovery was genuine or not, and whether it succeeded or not, it involved the Catholic concerned in considerable legal expenses. The question of the rent payable by a Catholic is not referred to as a major grievance, as far as my evidence goes. Rents for land rose during the century and continued to rise when the popery laws relating to property were repealed in 1778 and 1782. Even when rents were fixed at two-thirds of the annual value when a lease was executed, the fall in the value of money tended to reduce the proportion of the annual value payable by the tenant as the years passed. Catholics who had leases in reversion before the acts of 1704 and 1709 were never deprived of them.

century. This they did, moreover, despite strong competition and determined opposition from the substantial Protestant mercantile community in many of these towns.

The government of all the towns and cities was in hands of members of the Established Church and no Catholic could be admitted a freeman. In the years of bitterness which followed the treaty of Limerick Protestants in the towns jealously guarded the privileged position which they had temporarily lost during the reign of James II, and they constantly struck an alarmist note during the early years of the century. In 1704 the city council in Cork informed parliament that 'great numbers of Irish are flocking into the city to the great damage of the Protestant inhabitants by encroaching on their respective trades'. Catholics were said to be engaging to a considerable extent in foreign trade, because of their connections with Catholic countries abroad, thereby exciting the jealousy of Protestants, who, no doubt, greatly exaggerated the extent of Catholic participation in this branch of trade.[3] In 1709 the Cork Council was trying to forward a movement among the other cities and towns to demand legislation which would prohibit Catholics completely from carrying on a foreign trade. In 1737 a Cork pamphleteer, calling himself Alexander the Coppersmith, warned Catholic

[3] It is of interest to note that George Berkeley, Protestant bishop of Cloyne, in *The Querist* (1750) draws attention to what he considers the unwise policy of permitting Catholics to amass wealth in trade, while prohibiting them from owning land. He asks: 'Whether the sea-ports of Galway, Limerick, Cork and Waterford are not to be looked on as keys of this kingdom? And whether the merchants are not possessed of these keys; and who are the most numerous merchants in those towns?' Berkeley was a detached observer of the Irish scene, with a great desire to improve the economy of the country. His testimony to the numerical strength of Catholic merchants in these cities reinforces to some extent that of the Protestant freemen.

traders that parliament would restrain them if they continued 'their bold monopoly of home and foreign trade'. He complained of Catholic correspondence with countries abroad, and of French galleys coming into Cork consigned to Catholic merchants, and he declared that Catholics would, if not prevented, 'swallow up the trade and suck the marrow' of Cork. He accused them of always dealing with each other and always employing each other, and averred that 'if a Papist at the gallows wanted an ounce of hemp, he'd skip the Protestant shops, and run to Mallow Lane to buy it.' An attempt had been made in 1704 to limit the Catholic population of Limerick and Galway, but it had proved entirely unsuccessful. A petition from the corporation of Galway presented to parliament in 1762 stated that of the 14,000 inhabitants only 350 were Protestants. Protestants were, they complained, 'discouraged from following trade or business; Papists in general declining to deal with them; and the wealth of the town, or by much the greater part of it, being in their hands, they thereby acquired considerable influence and power over the indigent Protestant tradesmen.' In Limerick also the greater part of the trade of the city was in their hands, the richest Catholic merchants being the Roches and the Arthurs. The Roches were among the richest merchants in the south of Ireland. They built an enormous warehouse on the quays and had their own ships mounted with guns for the West India trade.

It was naturally galling for the Protestants of Cork, Waterford, Limerick and Galway and other towns to see Catholics flourishing in spite of the popery laws, and in direct contravention of the rules and regulations and traditions of government in cities and chartered towns. According to the charters only guild members were free to carry on trade, and since all Catholics were denied admission to the guilds Catholic traders could be obstructed and all goods offered for sale by them were liable to confiscation. It proved impossible to enforce the terms of the charters, however, in a situation where the majority of customers were Catholic, and inclined to act together in opposition to Protestants. There was no law to compel Catholics to buy in Protestant shops, hence efforts to monopolize trade were doomed to failure. Catholics could always have set up in business immediately outside the town boundaries, as they did, for instance, in St. Francis Abbey, outside the walls of Limerick, and gradually new towns could have been created completely outside the jurisdiction of guilds and corporations. To meet this situation the guilds had already, in the last quarter of the seventeenth century, permitted Catholics to become second-class guild members. They were permitted to become quarter-brothers in the guilds, i.e. members from quarter to quarter, and they were free to trade so long as they paid their dues to the guilds and conformed to guild regulations. The status of quarter-brother, however, carried no privileges or rights apart from trading rights, and control of affairs in the cities and towns remained exclusively in Protestant hands. After the treaty of Limerick there had been a strong movement in the guilds to prevent quarter-brothers from taking any apprentices at all, but these attempts had to be abandoned when the popery law of 1704 decreed that Catholics might have two apprentices.

By the year 1717 the Catholics were already resisting the quarter-brother system. The resistance was probably not so much to the payment of quarterage, which was not an unduly heavy impost, but showed rather a determination on the part of Catholic merchants and traders to repudiate the claim of the guilds to decide whether or not they might carry on trade at all. As was to be expected, this movement took its rise in Cork, where Catholics were in a big majority. The right of the city authorities to imprison traders for refusing to pay quarterage to the guilds, was successfully challenged in the courts on the grounds that there was no statutory basis for the demand, and compensation had to be paid to Catholic traders in Cork, who had been imprisoned by order of the lord mayor. Soon Catholic resistance to paying quarterage spread to other cities and towns and in 1765 the councils and corporations of Cork, Limerick, Waterford, Dublin, Drogheda, Youghal, Clonmel, New Ross and Wexford all petitioned parliament asking for legislation which would confirm their right to give or withold permission to trade, and to be paid quarterage by traders who were non-guild members. The movement found much support in the house of commons and draft quarterage bills were passed in 1767, 1771, 1773 and 1778, but they were cushioned in the Irish privy council and the demand for quarterage never received the sanction of statute law. Catholics petitioned parliament against each of the quarterage bills, the Catholic Committee in Dublin acting as the centre of opposition to the measure. The Catholics of Cork, Dublin, Limerick, Drogheda, Clonmel, Enniskillen, Carrickfergus, Youghal, Waterford, Dungarvan, Cashel and Carrick-on-Suir all made a stand against the corporate authorities at this time. After 1778 the attempt to exact quarterage from Catholics was abandoned, and their right to freedom of trade was never again questioned. However, the Protestant corporations, whose members claimed to be foremost in defence of the Irish Protestant interest, remained the avowed opponents of Catholic aspirations throughout the eighteenth century, and indeed until the passing of the Municipal Reform Act of 1840.

From the early years of the eighteenth century the point had occasionally been made that the popery laws had tended to recoil on the ruling class themselves, and were a serious bar to economic advancement. This argument began to be heard more frequently as the Irish parliament became more independent in outlook, and particularly after 1750, began to make grants to assist manufacturers, to improve communications and to encourage tillage, forestry and fisheries and other types of private enterprise. Surprisingly enough, parliament in 1757 gave a grant of £4,000 to Thomas Wyse of the Manor of St. John in Waterford, a founder member, in 1760, of the Catholic Committee. This grant was to enable him to expand an industry he had established in Waterford for the manufacture of metal and plated ware. Some observers believed, and Catholic apologists – among them Charles O'Conor of Belanagare – who wished to make a case for repeal of the popery laws, continually asserted, that the very severe restrictions on Catholics with regard to mortgages and leases aggravated economic distress by discouraging capital investment among Catholics. It was estimated that they held a considerable share of the available money, and although, like the Jews, they became money-lenders, the risk was great, since they were not permitted to take landed security, and they were accordingly reputed to prefer foreign investment. Some members of parliament wished to see this money put into circulation in Ireland, in the interests of public and private credit, and attempts were made from 1762 on, to secure for Catholics the right to acquire mortgages and longer leases. It has been suggested, probably with some truth, that Catholic money-lenders brought pressure to bear on members of parliament who were indebted to them, to support these bills. Between the years 1762 and 1774 seven bills were introduced in the Irish parliament seeking to give Catholics permission to take mortgages on landed security, but they were bitterly opposed and failed to become law. Several bills introduced between 1746 and 1774 to enable Catholics to take longer leases met with similar opposition, although they included a clause whereby the leasehold interest should be gavelled or divided among the children as in the case of Catholic landed estates. The supporters of these lease bills contended that this clause would ensure that the Catholic commercial class, hitherto largely untouched by the popery laws, would find themselves under the same pressures as the Catholic landed gentry, and would conform to the Established Church rather than see their property whittled away in succeeding generations. The majority of Irish members of parliament, however, opposed all attempts to relax the popery laws, and they brought forward arguments to counter the claim that such bills would improve the country's economy. These measures, they said, instead of improving the economy, would encourage a drift to the towns; would subject Protestants to increased rents since there would be severe competition for land if Catholics were allowed longer leases; and moreover, the measures would lead Catholics to withdraw their money from trade and manufacture and from government loans.

Nevertheless, the years between 1768 and 1774 do mark a slight advance in the Catholic position, an advance which owed much to the force of the economic argument. During this period means were devised to provide secure investment facilities for Catholics in projects of national and public utility, which at the same time left the whole system of the popery laws intact. The earliest example I have found of this opening of the back door to Catholic investment was an act of 1768 for improving navigation between Limerick and Killaloe. To encourage Catholics to invest in the enterprise all shares were to be regarded as 'personal estate and not subject to any of the laws to prevent the growth of popery'. Thus the indirect ownership of land involved in such investment would not be at the mercy of Protestant discoverers. A blanket concession on similar lines was given in 1772 to Catholic shareholders in all inland navigation companies and in insurance companies. The fact that these acts now made it possible for Catholics to become shareholders and sometimes directors in such companies as the Grand Canal Company, must have served to break down segregation barriers to some slight extent.

Soon, however, events were to favour a more fundamental change in the Catholic position. The late 1770's saw the outbreak of the American war in which France was the ally of the rebellious colonists, and the ministry in England became convinced that some concessions must be made to Irish Catholics to ensure that Ireland should not become a weak point in the empire's defences. Pressure from England played an important part in getting a measure through the Irish parliament in 1778 permitting Catholics to take leases for 999 years. In 1782 another act was passed which enabled them to buy land outright. Catholics were now in a much better position to expand their business interests and to play a fuller part in the commercial life of the country, and it could probably be claimed that the increased prosperity, which was evident in Ireland for some years after 1782, owed not a little to these two Catholic relief acts. At the same time, the removal of the barriers against Catholic acquisition of landed property, and their admission to the professions in 1792 and 1793, changed to some extent the pattern of investment and the way of life of some wealthy Catholics. Hitherto they had led lives in which ostentation could play little part and their opportunities for lavish spending were circumscribed. The desire, so long suppressed, to cut a figure in society, was now given opportunities for satisfaction, and Catholic merchants and manufacturers tended to divert more money than perhaps they should, from their commercial interests, while in many instances their sons turned to the professions instead of entering the family business. It was unfortunate, perhaps, that in this way money and talent were withdrawn from commercial enterprises at the time of the union, when Ireland, for the first time, met the great challenge of free trade.

Although Catholics were now in position to increase their wealth and to play their part in bringing about an expansion in the Irish economy, they continued to feel aggrieved because of their exclusion from the upper echelons of commercial life. Catholics, for instance, had helped to raise funds for the building of the Royal Exchange in Dublin, yet no Catholic could be a trustee of the Royal Exchange. Neither were they permitted to become governors or directors of the Bank of Ireland. As well as this, the old feud between the Catholics and the Protestant corporations of the cities and towns was intensified in the early 1790s, when the corporations, led by Dublin corporation, took a prominent part in opposing the Catholic relief measures of 1792 and 1793. Although the act of 1793 permitted Catholics to become freemen of towns, it was found impossible to end discrimination by legislation, and the guilds and corporations continued to maintain their exclusively Protestant character. Even when Catholics were made eligible for corporation office by the relief act of 1829, legal eligibility made no change in the *de facto* position. The relief act was simply permissive and there was no obligation on the Protestant guilds and corporations to relinquish their monopoly, by admitting Catholics to the freedom or to corporate office. The exclusion of Catholics from town and city politics was virtually complete until the passing of the Municipal Reform Act in 1840. This act extinguished most of the smaller corporations and Catholics soon gained control in the majority of those which survived.

It would seem, however, that the Catholic commercial class greatly exaggerated the significance of their exclusion in the years before 1840. It is true that the freemen of cities and towns enjoyed not only a share in the elective franchise, but other very real advantages in such matters as exemption from tolls, tenancy of corporate property, water supply, credit, corporation contracts etc. in an age when patronage and preference, not to say graft, were practised openly. Denys Scully (a prominent Catholic spokesman before O'Connell became the recognised leader) in his *Statement of the Penal Laws*, published in 1812, presented a picture of the disadvantages experienced by Catholics in economic life, which is typical of the pro-emancipation propaganda of the period. He wrote:

> All Catholic merchants, tradesmen and artizans... are under the necessity... of residing in these cities and towns, and under the yoke of corporate power. Perhaps these men and their families amount in number to some *hundred thousands* of the most useful, laborious and valuable citizens of Ireland. Such persons in any well-regulated state, would be deemed fit objects of favour and encouragement, at least of protection. But, in Ireland, their lot is a grievous one. They are debased by the galling ascendancy of privileged neighbours. They are depressed by partial imposts; by undue preferences... bestowed upon their competitors;... by an uncertain and unequal measure of justice; by fraud and favouritism daily and openly practised to their prejudice... Every species of Catholic industry and mechanical skill is checked, taxed, and rendered precarious.

This was the case constantly made by politicians, and Daniel O'Connell campaigned vigorously, for much of his public life, against the Protestant monopoly of power in cities and corporate towns.

It is true that these charges were not without foundation, but it is not true that Catholics were prevented from prospering in business because of their exclusion from corporate office. When the government made £200,000 available for the support of public credit during the financial crisis of

1793, three of the seven commissioners appointed to supervise loans to traders and manufacturers, were Catholic merchants – John Ball, Valentine O'Connor and Edward Byrne of Mullinahack. Byrne, although a Catholic, had become the richest merchant in Dublin by the end of the century, despite the fact that he was not a freeman of Dublin, that he could not be a trustee of the Royal Exchange nor a director of the Bank of Ireland. He died reputedly worth £400,000, and if the firm collapsed in the next generation, it was not because of anti-Catholic laws, but because Byrne's sons did not inherit their father's business ability.

The desire of Catholics to challenge the Protestant stranglehold on municipal government led their leaders to make political capital by attributing economic stagnation to religious discrimination. Scully makes the claim that:

...the peculiar misery of Irish corporate towns; the general ignorance and unskilfulness of their tradesmen; their dear charges for labour; their irrational combinations; their abject poverty; their squalid exterior... are solely attributable to this perverted and unnatural system of penal laws, which confounds all ordinary principles of human action, and frustrates the most helpful projects of benevolence and patriotism.

The truth is that the misery and squalor of Dublin in 1812 were no more attributable to penal laws than they were a hundred years later, at the time of the lock out of 1913, when Catholics had a great deal of power in Dublin corporation.

In the early years of the nineteenth century Catholic leaders constantly asserted that lawlessness in Ireland as revealed by combinations in cities and by the activities of agrarian secret societies in rural districts, could only be eradicated by granting Catholics full religious equality. They used the unrest which was generated by the poverty and the economic grievances of the mass of the population to advance the social, economic and political aspirations of a relatively small number of wealthy Catholics. A similar pattern has evolved in other countries whether discrimination has rested on religious, class or racial grounds, and it would have been unusual indeed had Catholic landlords and Catholic employers in Ireland combined in assuming responsibility for bettering the conditions of their co-religionists. Nevertheless, it is unfortunate that the population was divided into two warring camps – one claiming perpetual ascendancy and the other determined to achieve equality – and that energy was dissipated in this sectarian struggle, which might have been better used, had leaders on both sides been willing to unite in seeking a solution to the country's economic problems.

IV

CAPITAL IN THE IRISH ECONOMY

BY

J. Lee

It is still widely believed that lack of capital was a serious obstacle to economic development in nineteenth-century Ireland. Though vehemently expressed by almost all politic-ians at the time, this view was rejected by most informed commentators. As early as 1798, one observer bluntly claimed that 'want of capital is more frequently complained of than felt; it is in many cases the argument by which indolence endeavours to justify inactivity'. In 1838 the famous coachman, Charles Bianconi, agreed with G. A. Hamilton, Chairman of the Dublin & Drogheda Railway, that though very large concentrations of capital might be few in Ireland, yet there was abundant unused capital lying idle in smaller amounts. A decade later, the academic economists, Professor Longfield, Professor Hancock and Robert Kane concurred in the view of the practical bankers, Jonathan and James Pim, that there was an actual surplus of capital in relation to the demand for it. It is noteworthy that English insurance and railway companies, well aware that there was capital in Ireland, advertised their shares in Irish papers and appointed agents in various towns to tap the potential supply. The available statistics strongly support this viewpoint. By 1860 about £40,000,000 of Irish money was invested in British government stock, and another £20,000,000 was on deposit in the Irish joint stock and savings banks.

Even £60,000,000 lying idle may not sound a very large sum until it is realised what a remarkably small amount of capital was required by manufacturing industry. It was investment in the infrastructure, not in the manufacturing sector, that ate up capital – investment in roads, canals, railways, docks, ships, houses. Dublin alone invested more money in railways between 1844 and 1850 than Belfast invested in the fixed capital of the linen industry in the whole of the preceeding fifty years. Ironically, the large quantities of capital necessary for the infrastructure, and for joint stock enterprise in general, were usually forthcoming, if occasionally after some delay. The reluctance to invest was not due to lack of savings – Ireland saved far more capital than she invested at home, but this capital was rarely risk capital. It only slowly found its way into even joint stock companies, as the experience of the banks and the railways clearly shows, until English money came in first and bore the initial risk. Parliament abolished the Bank of Ireland monopoly of joint stock banking in 1821. But except in Belfast there was no immediate effort to form new banks because of a clause in the 1821 Act requiring all shareholders to be resident in Ireland. As Irish investors lacked the confidence to subscribe to companies in which there was no English capital, this was tantamount to a continued prohibition of joint stock banking in the south of Ireland. Once this particular clause was repealed new banks were established after 1824, and when they began to pay good dividends Irish investors, as in the case of the National Bank and the Royal, bought out the English shareholders within fifteen years.

Railway investment followed the same pattern. In 1843 the promotors of the Great Southern & Western Railway tried to raise a million pounds in Dublin, but received little support. In the spring of 1844, however, many of the shares were taken up in London, and when this became known in Dublin there was an immediate rush to invest in the company. About one third of the total capital was subscribed in

Dublin in 1844 and 1845, and, even more significantly, once the company began to pay dividends after 1850, Irish investors, as in the case of the banks earlier, bought out the English shareholders. In 1861, 76 per cent of the shares were held in Ireland compared with only 35 per cent in 1851. Earlier still, in the 1830's, the very first Irish railway, the Dublin & Kingstown, could not have been built without government assistance, while at the same time the shares allotted to Ireland by the London & Birmingham railway were being snapped up instantly, though in the event the Dublin & Kingstown paid equally good dividends as the London & Birmingham. These examples show that, as the agent of the English Globe insurance company put it in 1835, it was not capital, but confidence, that Irish investors lacked.

The infrastructure absorbed the largest amounts of capital. Next in importance, especially when working capital is taken into account, were export traders, particularly grain and butter traders early in the nineteenth century, and, increasingly after 1830, cattle traders. Apart from occasional short-term difficulties, there is no evidence of any underlying lack of capital to finance exporters. The real problem arises in examining the supply of capital to industry. Most manufacturing was carried on, not by joint stock concerns, but by private family businesses which did not seek capital from the general public. We must therefore look closely at the family business – or rather at the business family – to understand the role of capital in industry. By far the most important source of fixed capital in family firms in all countries is reinvestment of profits. And it was precisely this ploughing back of profits into continued expansion that was most lacking in Ireland. Numerous observers drew attention to the haemorrhage of capital out of business and into the professions and land. Arthur Young complained in the 1770's of business people 'quitting trade or manufactures, when they have made £5,000 or £10,000 to become gentlemen', while, a century later, Thomas Keating, a Scottish businessman, argued that 'a man accumulates in Ireland a few thousands, and if he keeps them he does not invest them; in England or Scotland his sons would consider that just a good foundation for developing an industry or business... in Ireland the sons want to be professional men... the father dies and the business ceases. That is a very common thing in Ireland, because in the higher classes there is a vulgar contempt for work, and with those who aspire to mingle with them, the same contempt for work obtains. The first thing an Irish man of the upper middle classes does is to get out of any connection with business the moment he can'. The charge is exaggerated, but it is nonetheless true that many business families viewed business as a halfway house on the way to a higher and better way of life among the professional or landed classes. Business was felt to be all very well for a man on the make, but not for a made man. And apart altogether from the question of social prestige, there were sometimes sound economic reasons for preferring a professional or landed income to a business one – it was often higher, and usually more certain. There are many examples of brewers in the 1830's and 40's bleeding their businesses dry to purchase estates for £40,000, their businesses consequently declining for lack of working capital. Even Guinnesses almost failed in the 1820's, partly because of their very low investment rate in the previous decade when they had abstracted capital from the firm to buy a large amount of government stock. This strongly developed tendency to extract capital from industry helps explain some of the more puzzling phenomena of nineteenth-century Ireland, such as the very rapid turnover of firms – only four of the thirty-eight coachmaking firms in Dublin in 1800 survived among the twenty-five coachmakers of 1850 – the exceptionally large number of professional people, and the remarkable speed with which the encumbered estates were gobbled up by middle class buyers once they came on the market after 1850. In a country allegedly short of capital, abundant capital was available to buy into landed society. Ironically, families retired from business not because they lacked capital, but because they had acquired capital. Notable exceptions were the Quakers, who were distinguished less by their ability to found firms than by the simple fact that they remained in business, and in the Belfast area, where the aristocratic cult never took as deep root as in the south.

To what extent could it be argued that, because of the lack of a market, there was no opportunity for investment in Ireland, that it was not the supply of, but the demand for capital from manufacturing industry that was too small? This, I think, is true up to a point, but while the lack of a market would explain why firms could not be founded, it does not explain why they should be wound up. Irish manufacturers did suffer severely from English competition, but this in itself points to the existence of a market. What is true is that the nature of the home market was changing rapidly after 1850, but change meant expansion as well as contraction, expansion for which many Irish manufacturers were not psychologically prepared, as a remarkable letter from James Winstanley in 1885 shows. Winstanley describes how in shoe manufacturing, the bench system was replacing the old hand sewn methods, and, as Irish manufacturers were backward in adopting the new system, English competition was becoming ever more serious. 'It may be urged', he continued, 'that if such goods have obtained a hold on the Irish market, the best way to meet it is to have them made in Ireland. It is to be observed, however, that the rivalry between Irish and other makers is not one of cheapness, but one of quality. No Irish manufacturer has yet attempted the experiment of putting out a still worse boot than his cross-channel opponent, for of course cheapening means reduction in quality. It is the best feature of the Irish trade that there is no ambition to supplant imported rubbish by rubbish of home manufacture'. After this extraordinary outburst, it is impossible to feel much sympathy for him when he goes on to blame the shopkeepers for 'introducing and selling to their customers the very lowest class of boots and shoes'. What was happening here was not that the market was contracting, but that it was expanding, that a new class of customers was buying its footwear in shops for the first time, and that when Irish manufacturers turned up their noses at serving such humble feet, English manufacturers took their chance.

It has been frequently claimed that the Irish market was reduced in size by political manipulation, firstly through the effects of the Act of Union, and then by absentee rents and excessive taxation, both of which drained capital from the country and reduced the size of the market. Let us examine these points in turn. The contention that manufacturers were discouraged from investing because the emigration of aristocratic families destroyed their market is unconvincing. The migration of these families caused unemployment and hardship among those who catered for their wants − but these wants were for luxury goods for conspicuous consumption, carpets, wigs, liveries, furniture, dresses. This was a narrow, limited, selective clientele. The Industrial Revolution depended on getting away from this type of good, catering to the cheap wants of thousands of consumers, on mass production for a mass market. There is no recorded case of an industrial revolution based on the fashion industry, and the migration of these aristocratic families had a very limited impact indeed on the development of the home market. The absentee argument is equally unconvincing. Absentee rents accounted for about

£2,000,000 per annum throughout most of the nineteenth century, but there was little difference in the economic role of absentee and ordinary rents. A large portion of rents went to meet the annual debt on mortgages held by English or Dublin insurance companies, or was spent on imported luxuries. In neither case did they stimulate investment in Ireland. The difference between ordinary and absentee rents was that the former were presented to the landlord in Ireland, who then himself transferred them out of the country, whereas the latter were delivered directly to the landlord in England. The difference was merely between a direct or an indirect transfer of money abroad. The argument would be more convincing if it were directed, not against absentee rents, but against rents in general, which represented a total loss to any productive use of at least 10 per cent of the national income. In view of the fact that landowners, who, theoretically, could have saved most, in fact saved least, the high rate of saving in the economy to which we have already alluded becomes even more astonishing. There was in fact probably too much saving in the second half of the nineteenth century, money being diverted from consumption into deposits which the banks then transferred to England, thus reducing domestic consumption without increasing investment.

Overtaxation was the third standard Irish complaint, particularly after Gladstone imposed heavier rates on whiskey after 1853. The taxation of Ireland question was partly a taxation of whiskey question, though the other standard luxuries of the poor, tea and tobacco, were also heavily taxed. Gladstonian taxation was regressive, it penalised the poor, and as the proportion of poor was higher in Ireland than in England, the relative taxation of Ireland was also higher. Taxation was a question of classes, not of countries, or, as Nassau Senior put it, 'Ireland is not so much poor because she is over taxed as over taxed because she is poor.'

Lower taxation would not have led directly to higher capital formation, because the poor would have spent rather than invested the extra money available to them, perhaps on more whiskey, on more tea, on more tobacco, but perhaps also on other consumer goods, some of which might have been supplied within the Irish economy.

With so many relatively small capitals in the economy it was essential that they should be collected and channelled into the most productive employment. Following the ending of the Bank of Ireland's monopoly in 1821 most of the banks whose names are familiar today – the Provincial, the National, the Northern, the Ulster, the Royal, the Hibernian, were established and, as the century wore on, collected a growing proportion of the community's savings, until by 1914 total bank deposits amounted to nearly £60,000,000. As the banks, however, channelled this money out of the country, it is questionable whether the most productive possible use was made of it from the national viewpoint. For Irish banking was so closely modelled on the British pattern that the concept of investment banking, as developed on the continent after 1830, never really caught on here. The difference between the normal joint stock and the investment bank can be very crudely summed up as that the joint stock banker waited for businessmen to apply to him, while the investment banker established firms himself with the bank's funds. English banking suited the English economy, blessed as it was with a horde of private entrepreneurs; unfortunately the Irish economy differed considerably from the English. Ireland had the advanced English concept of banking applied to a relatively poor economy. However, at the very worst, the banking system was merely a contributory factor, and far from being the most important one in the mis-allocation of Irish capital. Its conservatism reflected rather than created the general tone of business life.

The banks were criticised even more vehemently for their alleged failure to assist agriculture. The farmers had to provide most of their own investment capital, and this investment, as can be seen from the rise in livestock numbers after 1830, was quite substantial. The small farmer's reluctance to resort to outside sources of capital was often justified, for he found it expensive to borrow from the banks, whose credit policies were not primarily adapted to his rather unremunerative requirements. On the other hand, there is little evidence of an overall scarcity of capital in agriculture after 1850, however hard pressed individual farmers may have been at times, and a good deal of borrowing was by inefficient farmers for consumption rather than investment. It was a widely noted phenomenon that while substantial amounts earmarked for dowries lay on deposit at two per cent, the farmer borrowed at ten per cent or complained he couldn't borrow at all. It is questionable to what extent the dowry system abstracted capital from agriculture – some dowries were invested in the farm, but many went to pay off emigrant brothers and sisters. Emigrant remittances compensated for the capital taken out of the country in emigrants' pockets, but not for the expenditure on the emigrant by the community until he reached emigrant age, most of which was wholly unproductive expenditure from the economic viewpoint. In general the problem of capital in agriculture was much the same as in industry, not the absolute amount, but its intelligent and productive application, not the quantity, but the quality.

The British government is frequently blamed for not having undertaken large-scale investment in Ireland. On balance, the government extracted more money from the country than it ploughed back, though it did in fact invest modestly, particularly through the Board of Works after 1831, in canals, railways, roads and drainage. Some of this investment was squandered. The canals, heavily subsidised, could have been built at half the cost, and government subsidies, whether Irish in the eighteenth century or British in the nineteenth, were partly wasted. Drainage and reclamation projects were sometimes successful, though often, as at Pobol O'Keefe, attempted on unsuitable land. The fisheries were given grants in dribs and drabs, on an on-again, off-again system. With public as with private capital, it was not that the absolute amount was too small, but that bad planning led to it being wastefully used from the national viewpoint. And of course government intervention under the Union was confined to infrastructure; it steered completely clear of manufacturing industry.

Ireland was an exporter of capital for much of the nineteenth century, and many Irish writers regarded it as a virtual breach of the Act of Union that the English capital which Pitt promised did not flow to Ireland. Though Pitt's forecasts proved false, the complaint is based, from an economic viewpoint, on a misunderstanding. English investment in the nineteenth century, both at home and abroad, was concentrated heavily on railways, government stock and mines. As we have seen, English money did flow into similar Irish enterprises, frequently earlier than Irish money. Ireland was not discriminated against in terms of British investment; she was a normal, not an exceptional, case.

This survey has emphasised that Ireland suffered less from a shortage of capital than from the wasteful use of capital by savers, investors, businessmen, in other words, that Ireland's human capital failed to make the best use of the country's resources. Human capital can be best developed and fostered through education, and while universal growth, it was indispensable, however, that the best use should be made of the money invested in education. But much talent was wasted, both because too few able students were allowed go on for higher education, and because a great deal of that education was, in any event, irrelevant to the economic needs of the country, so that while, for instance, there was a serious shortage of veterinary surgeons, the Four Courts swarmed with briefless barristers. There is no more evidence of a lack of capital in Ireland today than a century ago. But its use presents a continuing challenge, and the lesson of the nineteenth century, for this country as for many others, may be that the amount of capital itself is less important than the quality of the country's human capital – its farmers labour force, businessmen and administrators.

V

POPULATION GROWTH AND THE IRISH ECONOMY

Michael Drake

During the last two centuries the population of every country of the Western World has grown faster than ever before with one exception – Ireland. Today the population of Ireland is about four and one quarter millions, little bigger than it was two hundred years ago. In that time England's population has grown sixfold; so has that of the Netherlands. There are now four times as many Norwegians as in 1800 and three times as many Swedes. Even France, a country with a notoriously sluggish rate of population growth, has twice as many inhabitants as on the eve of the French Revolution. To trace the course of Ireland's remarkable population history over these last two hundred years is to come close to the springs of her social and economic life.

If we go back to the beginning of the eighteenth century we find Ireland was very much like all other Western countries. The vast majority of her population, like theirs, were engaged in agriculture. Living standards were low compared with those of today but were probably not very different from those in most other European countries. At this time all populations suffered sharp set-backs at frequent intervals; largely as a result of bad harvests or epidemics or war. A famine in Finland, for example, during the years 1696–97 is estimated to have killed 30% of the population. To go back a little further, we find the population of Denmark declined by as much as 20% during the 1650s. We haven't the neces-

65

sary statistical information to determine whether or not Ireland's population experienced reverses of this order. Nevertheless, we can be fairly certain that death was ever present and that most Irishmen lived close to the margin of subsistence. As the eighteenth century progressed, however, so did Ireland. About the middle of the century her population began to grow at first rather slowly, about 5% every decade, but increasing, so that by the end of the century it was rising by possibly as much as 15% a decade; sufficient for it to double in 50 years. This population growth was in line with that of other Western countries, perhaps being a little faster than in most.

Why the Irish population should begin to grow at this time and at this speed remains, however, something of a mystery. Professor Connell of Queen's University, Belfast, has argued that the main cause was a striking fall in the age of marriage which led to a rise in the birth rate. The main reason advanced for this fall in the marriage age is that towards the end of the eighteenth century it became easier to get a holding big enough to support a family. This was because Irish men and women were prepared to live almost exclusively on potatoes, a crop providing far more nourishment per acre than any kind of grain or other foodstuff. Furthermore, from the middle of the eighteenth century the external demand for Irish agricultural products grew sharply. This, Professor Connell suggests, encouraged the landlords to create numerous small tenancies in the hope of increasing their rent rolls. Under rack-renting landlordism the Irish farmer derived no benefit from delaying marriage and once he had got a holding he could, by accepting the potato as his staple food, contemplate the creation of a large family without fear of starvation.

Whether in fact the age at marriage did or did not fall remains an open question. It is true that many contemporaries thought the average Irishman married early. Reports of marriage for both men and women taking place in the late teens are common. Unfortunately, most of these reports are anecdotal and impressionistic and on matters like this such evidence is usually very inaccurate indeed: coloured far too often by the prejudices of the observer. For many people thought the lower classes, and not just in Ireland, married recklessly without a thought for the future and at far too early an age. Yet whenever we can check these impressions against statistical evidence we find the earliness of marriage is much exaggerated. For example, the consensus of opinion amongst a variety of witnesses appearing before the Irish Poor Enquiry Commission in the 1830s was that the usual age at marriage of men in Connaught was about 19 years. However, when the Census Commissioners in 1841 looked into the matter they produced a set of statistics showing that the average age at marriage was unlikely to have been under 25 years at any time during the 1830s. In other words, the statistics showed that men married at least six years later than contemporaries, basing their conclusions on impressionistic evidence only, believed to be the case.

My own view on the cause of the growth in population in eighteenth-century Ireland is that it came about through a fall in the death rate, and I think the main reason for this fall is that food supplies expanded, principally through an increased cultivation of potatoes. The acceptance of the potato as the main component in the average diet meant that a growing population could be fed more adequately than if it were dependent on grain or animal products. For the potato demands relatively little labour and can be grown on land that would be unsuitable for grain. Furthermore, on a given acreage it will sustain twice as many people as would wheat. Potatoes, indeed, if eaten in sufficient quantities, are a very fine source of nourishment providing virtually everything the body needs; calories, protein, vitamins, trace elements, and if accompanied by a pint of milk a day can hardly be faulted, except perhaps on palatability.

There is, however, a third possible explanation of this quickening in the rate of population growth; some factor which applied not only in Ireland but throughout Europe, for as I mentioned earlier populations were growing in other parts of the continent. In this case the spread of a potato diet would have been the accompaniment rather than the cause of population growth. The population of Finland, for example, doubled between 1750 and 1800, a faster rate of growth than that of Ireland. England's population grew by 50% in the same period. In neither country can the increase be ascribed to the potato, whether acting upon the birth rate or the death rate. Perhaps then we should look for some entirely different reason, such as the spread of inoculation against smallpox, a practice that is reported to have been widespread in both Ireland and England in the late eighteenth century, as well as in other parts of Europe. Or perhaps some of the killer diseases, typhus and dysentery, lost some of their power, for diseases themselves can sicken and die, or the agents that carry them, rats and lice for instance, may suffer a setback.

For whatever reasons the population of Ireland certainly grew rapidly during the closing decades of the eighteenth century and the opening decades of the nineteenth. By 1840 it had topped the 8 million mark. This growth was accompanied by a striking expansion of the Irish economy. From the 1740s ever-increasing quantities of Irish animal products, particularly butter, pork and beef, went to satisfy the export market. Beginning in the 1770s Ireland also began to export grain in growing quantities and by the 1830s was sending abroad some 400,000 tons, most of it to England. This was enough to feed some 2 million people throughout an entire year. Ireland's exports were not confined to agricultural products however. The linen industry concentrated in the north developed at a spanking pace. Exports rose from under 3 million yards of linen cloth in 1720 to almost 7 million by 1740, 13 million in 1760 and 40 million by the end of the century. The expansion did not stop there. By 1835 some 70 million yards of linen cloth were being exported annually. Without the growth of population this achievement would not have been possible.

Much of the wealth created by the rising export trade did not benefit the mass of the population. Much went to the landlords, in the form of increased rents. It would be wrong, however, to think that Irish living standards were not improved. The customs books reveal very large and increasing quantities of tea, sugar and tobacco coming into the country, commodities which are usually taken to indicate a shift in the standard of living. It is, of course, true that by English standards Ireland was backward indeed, but so was every other country in Europe. England at this time was unique. English living standards were higher and the rate of growth of the English economy in the late eighteenth and early nineteenth centuries faster than anywhere else.

But if Irish conditions were poor by English standards, they were very probably not much different from those in the other countries of Western Europe and better than those in Eastern Europe. Consider for example, these remarks of Arthur Young, the English agricultural expert who toured Ireland in the 1770s: 'The fields are scenes of pitiable management', he wrote, 'as the houses are of misery. It is not in the power of an English imagination to figure the animals that waited upon us here. Some things that call themselves women, but were in reality walking dung hills. The country has a savage aspect, the people almost as wild as the country and the town one of the most brutal filthy places that can be seen. Mud houses, no windows. The poor people seem poor indeed, the children terribly ragged. If possible worse clad than if with no clothes at all. As to shoes and stockings, they are luxuries. The poor people's habitations are not so good. They are miserable heaps of dirt, no glass and scarcely any light.' A typical comment, one might say, on eighteenth- or early nineteenth-century Ireland. In fact the extract was taken from Young's tour of France: France, the most powerful country in Europe at that time and one which Young visited a few years after his tour of Ireland. Young had seen much that shocked him in Ireland. All English observers did. In summing up his impressions, however, he felt bound to remark, and I quote him directly: 'upon the whole we may fairly determine that judging by those appearances and circumstances which have been generally agreed to mark the prosperity or declention of a country Ireland has, since the year 1748, made as great advances as could possibly be expected. Perhaps greater than any other country in Europe.' He also noted that the people of Ireland seemed well fed, better off, as he put it with their bellyful of potatoes than the Englishman with but half a bellyful of more varied food-stuffs.

There was, however, a cloud on the horizon: the growing dependence of the rising population upon potatoes. After 1815, agricultural prices in England fell sharply despite the corn laws which reduced the import of grain from countries other than Ireland and helped, therefore, to keep up, to some extent, both the prices paid to English and to Irish farmers. But still the population of Ireland grew and landlords were loath to reduce rents. Since the levels of technology were low there was little chance of increasing yields per acre. Practically speaking, the only way was for the farmer to increase the amount of land devoted to producing the crop that paid the rent at the expense of the land devoted to growing food for himself and his family. The only way he could beat falling prices then was to produce more. If not for the farmer at any rate for the cottier this meant an even greater dependence on the potato and on the type of potato which yielded well in good years but which was liable to be erratic in its yield. This was the infamous 'lumper' variety. It was becoming ever more difficult for the cottier to find the modest patch of ground needed to support a family.

The 1820s and the 1830s saw living standards declining. The volume of exports contined to grow but not the imports of those commodities, which as I said earlier, are usually taken to be good indicators of rising or falling living standards, namely sugar, tobacco and tea. Famines returned after a gap of eighty years. There were few years in the 1820s and 1830s when food shortages were not reported from one part of the country or another. Death rates rose. Emigrant ships began to fill. The rate of population growth fell sharply in the 1830's. In the 1840s largely as a direct or an indirect result of the potato famine of 1845–47 the population of Ireland actually declined by 20% although it was probably falling even before this. This failure of the potato harvest over the entire country brought starvation and in its trail fever. Public relief measures on an unprecedented scale came too late to save many from a slow and agonising death. The Western world was shocked by what had happened. Recriminations filled the air.

No one would wish to detract from the horror of those years but for the sake of understanding the general sweep of Irish population history it is necessary to get them in perspective. First of all it should be borne in mind that the mortality caused by the potato famine appeared the more appalling because it occured in a Europe that had all but got rid of such catastrophes a hundred years earlier. Had the famine occurred in the early eighteenth or the late seventeenth centuries, it might well have gone unnoticed by the outside world and by historians, if not by contemporary commentators in Ireland itself. I have already mentioned the mortality of 30% in 1696–97 in Finland and the loss of 20% of the Danish population in the 1650s, neither of which events have ever made much impact, if it has been known at all, outside these countries. Also, of course, by the 1840s, Europe was much more closely knit than in the seventeenth or early eighteenth centuries. Communications were much better. Ireland very quickly became news. But above all statistics were kept. The extent of the tragedy could be and was quantified. It is the absence of precise statistical information on the famines of earlier days that has led us to ignore them. Nevertheless, if we search the literature we can find accounts of famines and epidemics that might well have been no less devastating than that of 1845–47. Take for example the crisis of 1740–41, possibly the last major setback to Ireland's population growth in the eighteenth century, and, therefore, a significant, if much neglected, event. Comments like the following from a letter written in Cashel and dated May 25th, 1741 have a familiar ring for anyone conversant with the literature of the 1840s:

'Multitudes have perished and are daily perishing under hedges and ditches. Some of fevers, some of fluxes and some through downright cruel want in the utmost agonies of despair. I have seen the labourer endeavouring to work at his spade but fainting for want of food and forced to quit it. I have seen the aged father eating grass like a beast and in the anguish of his soul wishing for dissolution. I have seen the helpless orphan exposed on the dung hill and none to take him in for fear of infection. And I have seen the hungry infant sucking at the breast of the already expired parent.'

It is not surprising that this year 1741 should be known as *bliain an áir* or the year of the slaughter'. Such disasters disappeared from Ireland for almost a century. Hence the shock of the potato famine in the 1840s was all the greater because it was unexpected, even anachronistic.

Another feature of the great famine which seems to be misunderstood is the question of its inevitability. Traditionally we are led to believe that the Irish were bound to suffer something like the great famine because, through no fault of their own, they had been forced onto a diet containing virtually nothing but potatoes. Of course, without the potato there would have been no potato famine, but one should also remember that without the potato the death rate would in all probability have been very much higher than it was in early nineteenth-century Ireland. It effectually eradicated food shortages. Without the potato the population of Ireland may not have continued to grow as it did and in so far as the rising population contributed, through its impact on the labour market and in raising demand, to the growth of the economy, what prosperity Ireland enjoyed must to some degree be ascribed to it. The disease which struck the potato in the second half of the 1840s came from outside the country causing a crop failure of quite a different character from those of earlier years. It need not have come, certainly it need not have come just then.

What, we might well ask, would have happened to the population of Ireland and to the Irish economy if the fungus had not attacked the potatoes? There seems little doubt that in the long run it would have declined though probably not so fast. Small famines of the type familiar enough in the 1820s and 1830s would no doubt have continued; gradually and agonisingly a new equilibrium between population and resources would have been reached. The suffering this involved would have been spread out over a greater number of years and a greater number of people. For Ireland, even with a much more favourable political and social climate, was hardly likely to have had an industrial revolution in the nineteenth century. She had neither the coal nor iron likely to generate economic growth. She had limited capital, relatively modest industrial skills, and a society not very conducive to entrepreneurship, though all these obstacles might have been overcome if she had had iron or coal or both, as the example of Wales at this time shows. Without these basic resources she could not expect to turn herself into a little England. No other country in Europe with comparable resources managed it. Why should Ireland have been the exception? Furthermore, the market for agricultural products, particularly grain, was less and less likely to provide the stimulus it had done in the eighteenth and early nineteenth centuries, as competition in the English market increased and pastoral exports rose. As every schoolboy knows, a pastoral economy can support fewer people than an arable one.

Another factor which helped to reduce Ireland's population was the fact that the English and American economies offered far greater rewards to Irish labour, skills, capital and enterprise than Ireland could ever hope to do, and the entry into the labour markets of both these countries was relatively easy for the Irish man or woman and became easier as earlier emigrants paved the way and linguistic barriers fell. The fall in population itself discouraged new investment, and in turn contributed to a further decline. And since the emigrants were usually in the younger working age groups emigration helped to produce an age distribution weighted towards the older and more conservative, less dynamic members of the work force. As new openings failed to appear people wanting to get married and not prepared to wait to an advanced age for a job that would enable them to do so, emigrated.

Ireland then remained a largely agricultural economy with

an industrial enclave in the north-east. Her people became her most important export; since by going they released pressure on the land and by remitting part of their wages helped to raise living standards in Ireland. For those who remained fewer were able to get married at a reasonable age and more were forced to remain celibate for life. For contrary to other Western countries Irish marital fertility, that is to say the number of children produced by each marriage, remained high. This being so the only way to contain a potentially explosive population growth, especially with falling death rates, was for large numbers of Irishmen and women to delay their marriages to a comparatively late age and for a very considerable minority to remain celibate for life.

How potentially explosive the population situation was is not often recognised, but if Ireland had maintained the age at marriage at its pre-famine level, say an average age for men of 25 and for women 22, and allowed the same proportion of the population to marry as did at that time, then the crude birth rate would have been about 35 to 40 per thousand. Had there been no emigration and had the death rate fallen to the extent that it actually did during the second half of the nineteenth and the first half of the twentieth centuries, then today the population of Ireland would be around 50 million. The impossibility of Ireland being able to support a population of this size at the present day, given the technological possibilities of the last 100 years, is an indication of the options open to Ireland in the mid-nineteenth century. She could have maintained her population at a low standard of living with high death rates. This would have allowed her people to marry at a reasonable age (reasonable that is by Western standards) and have large numbers of children, for few would have survived to adulthood. Emigration would not have been necessary. Alternatively, Ireland could have cut the death rate by restricting the number of births and hence the number demanding a share in the resources of the country. To restrict births, she could, as did other Western countries, adopt birth control within marriage, thus allowing more people to marry by their mid-twenties and at the same time lightening the burden of dependency; that is to say, reducing the number of children per head of the working population. By doing this, by reducing the burden of dependency that is, resources which would have gone on supporting dependents could have been used for investments designed to increase output in the future, permitting a rise in living standards for an already existing population or spreading the increased wealth amongst a bigger population. Ireland did not, as we know, choose to contain her population in either of these ways, that is through a high death rate or birth control within marriage. Instead she chose to limit her population growth by delaying marriage and by denying it altogether to as many as a third of her men and a quarter of her women. For those not prepared to make this sacrifice, she offered emigration.

VI

THE RAILWAYS IN THE IRISH ECONOMY

BY

J. Lee

A Corkman observed in 1866 that 'there is nothing that seems so to civilise us and bring things forward as the opening of railways.' Historians, however, have been inclined to overlook the role of the railway in the economy, mainly, I think, because the coming of the railway coincided with the Famine. The first line, the six mile suburban Dublin & Kingstown was opened in 1834, but the backbone of the system was laid between 1845 and 1853, when Dublin was connected with Cork, Galway and Belfast, and consequently we tend to attribute wholly to the Famine many of the subsequent changes which were partly due to the railway. The striking developments in rural diet between 1850 and 1900 – the increasing substitution, for instance, of Indian meal and bread for potatoes, of that strong black tea which the fastidious palates of travellers found so difficult to swallow for milk and water, the great increase in tobacco consumption, the change-over from home-spun to imported manufactured clothes, especially among women – were greatly facilitated by cheap railway transit to distribute the imports down the country. Without the railway, the post office could not have introduced cheap rates for mail order catalogues, nor would the army of commercial travellers that over-ran the country in the late nineteenth century have been nearly as large. Taken individually, all these may seem small matters. But when summed up, it is precisely these changes in rural diet and dress, in the range of choice of consumer goods and in knowledge of the outside world that distinguished the quality of living in Ireland in 1900 from that of 1850.

To appreciate the impact of the railway, we must realise that high transport costs were one of the main factors leading to the isolation of rural Ireland from the mainstream of economic life before 1850. It is true that Ireland had a fine road system, but roads catered primarily for passengers and light goods, not for long distance traffic in bulk goods. Irish roads were generally reckoned superior to English ones in the eighteenth and early nineteenth centuries, but the roads, excellent though they were, did not allow the carriage of bulk traffic at competitive rates, and before the railways, it was canals rather than roads that were necessary to open up the interior to sustained trade in bulk products. As the Drummond Report explained in 1838, 'the inland towns are only important in proportion as they offer good markets... and it is, in almost every instance, to the facilities afforded by a navigation they owe their superiority'. There could be no more revealing indication of the inadequacy of the transport system than the paltry 600 miles of navigable inland waterway in 1830 compared with England's 4,000. As late as 1847, even as the old pre-railway order collapsed, an experienced observer inspecting the Great Southern & Western route from Dublin to Cork noted that, because of the absence of water transport, 'for the general exchange of commodities, the interior of this part of Ireland is virtually more remote than India or America'.

The railway transformed this situation almost overnight. Railway rates varied widely for different classes of goods, but in general worked out at 2d per ton per mile, much the same as by canal, the railway of course being much faster. Where speed was not important, as with heavy goods like turf, bricks, malt and grain, canals remained competitive with railways. In 1853, James Perry, an outstanding Quaker railwayman, still thought that 'the canal ought to be the waggon, and the railway the coach or carriage of the country', and as late as 1890 canal traffic was higher than in 1840. True, the canals had to improve their services to meet the competition. In 1845, Charles Wye Williams, the largest carrier on the Grand Canal, actually supported a competing railway on the grounds that 'there is nobody wants competition more than they do', forecasting in mixed metaphors, 'they will no longer be the slow coach of the country'. Williams was right, railway competition jerked the Grand Canal into frantic activity, rates being reduced and the Canal becoming its own carrier in 1850. It would be ironic if the main impact of the railway was to compel an improvement in canal services. And, of course, the railways' contribution was not so much in reducing transport costs along canal banks, or close to the east coast, but in opening up hitherto isolated areas to the influence of the market. Even allowing, for argument's sake, that canals could have done as good a job, the fact remains that 3,000 miles of railway were built compared with a few hundred of canals.

The railway shortened the journey for passengers by over half, the steam engines chugging along at over 20 m.p.h. compared with less than 10 by coach or car, and the cost of travel was reduced by at least half. Most third class costs were in fact reduced fourfold, for the poor travelled mainly by special trains on market days, by excursion trains during the holiday season, and by the special harvest trains which the Midland Great Western ran for seasonal harvesters from Connaught to Britain. As late as 1914, however, excluding commuters in suburban areas, most people saw the inside of a train only once or twice a year. Before that, as one chairman put it, 'emigrants probably afford more traffic when they are leaving the country than when remaining in it'.

Historians of European economies regard the railway as a

powerful engine of economic development for three main reasons. Firstly, the railway generated expansion in the coal, iron and engineering industries, secondly, it brought hitherto inaccessible areas into the market economy, and thirdly it developed new export sectors. Let us look at these three factors in Ireland.

The sad, simple fact of course is that Ireland had no coal or iron. Steam engine manufacturers like Grendons of Drogheda, and wagon manufacturers like James Fagan of Dublin, had capacity orders in the boom building years from 1846 to 1848, but on the whole, British firms reaped the rewards of the investment generated by Irish railway demands. About one third of the total cost of construction of £45,000,000 between 1830 and 1914 was spent on imported iron and timber, the other two thirds mainly on land and labour. The contractors, of whom the greatest was William Dargan, paid £4,000,000 in wages between 1845 and 1850 alone. In ordinary circumstances this would make a spectacular addition to money incomes, but it was dwarfed by the £9,000,000 spent by the government on Famine relief. Similarly, the direct employment created by the railways – 20,000 of the most secure and sought after jobs in the country in 1900 – though substantial in its own right, could make little impact on the mass of Irish poverty.

The only industry that the railway could directly develop was tourism, which the companies did much to foster, building hotels along the west coast, subsidising races and regattas, developing the Curragh, helping organize the various Dublin and Cork exhibitions since 1853, distributing thousands of tourist guides and arranging through-rates to Irish resorts with British companies. Killarney, in particular, developed under the fosterage of the Great Southern & Western company. At a more modest level, holiday and residential areas were opened up by local lines from Dublin to Kingstown and later to Bray, Waterford to Tramore, Cork to Passage, Belfast to Holyhead and Bangor, Newry to Warrenpoint, but all this, while increasing the profits of local shopkeepers, was a far cry from the creation of burgeoning new industrial centres like Middlesboro or Furness. It is symptomatic that the first English railway, the Stockton & Darlington, was a coal line, whereas the Dublin & Kingstown, brilliantly managed though it was by James Pim, the Quaker father of Irish railways, relied mainly on suburban and pleasure traffic.

With the single exception of tourism, however, improved transport merely removed an obstacle to growth; it could not itself generate growth, which depended on the response of other sectors, and especially agriculture, to the new opportunities offered. True, the Midland Great Western tried to help the Galway fishing industry, and made an abortive attempt to establish a dead meat trade in pigs by setting up an abattoir in Dromod in 1884, but this was not really tackling the problem. Agriculture does not automatically imply backwardness. Ireland's basic problem, in 1860 as in 1960, was not that her economy was based on agriculture, but that it was based on extensive rather than intensive agriculture. The railway helped increase agricultural exports, which tripled in value between 1840 and 1914. English railways also contributed to this expansion. Transport costs between, say, Liverpool and Sheffield were as relevant to the Irish dealer as costs between Mullingar and Dublin. Already in the 1840's, the Newcastle & Carlisle created a market for Ulster livestock in the north of England; 'an Irishman', it was said, 'always puts his pigs on the railway'. But, English or Irish, the railways fitted into and accentuated the existing pattern; they did not transform the existing economic structure from agricultural to industrial. If anything, they contributed to the decline in the intensiveness of agriculture by facilitating the transition from tillage to pasture as English meat prices rose relative to bread prices after 1840. Cattle could now be exported much more conveniently, and carcase weights increased rapidly between 1840 and 1860 as the railway cut out the wearing journey to the sea ports along the drove roads, most of the reduction in transport costs going into the farmers' pockets. The impetus given to live as distinct from dead stock exports by the steam ship after 1825 was further strengthened by the railway. But all this was merely a shift of emphasis within agriculture. The peasant remained a peasant – or became an emigrant.

The railway did not industrialise the peasant – it in fact often had the effect of undermining existing local industry – but by widening the area under production for the market, it banished the reality, if not the spectre, of famine. But though living standards rose, the railway, by bringing knowledge of the outside world in its wake, ensured that aspirations rose more rapidly, and thus contributed to that revolution of rising expectations which is a prerequisite for progress in underdeveloped areas. All this was widely acknowledged by contemporaries, and yet by 1870 few had a good word to say about the railways, and by 1900 the dissatisfaction had swollen into a chorus of complaint. Why was this?

Firstly, it was alleged that lines were not built to a central plan, but had been put together bit by bit and did not follow the best routes. It is quite true that there was no central plan, but despite the piece-meal method of selection, most railways did follow sensible routes, and none of the overall master plans proposed in the 1830's and 40's were markedly superior to the system that eventually emerged. The Drummond Commission, for instance, specially appointed in 1836 to advise on the best system, produced a brilliant report on the state of the economy but proposed a quite unsatisfactory railway system, and when Barry O'Brien claimed in 1908 that its predictions about probable dividends had been remarkably accurate, he overlooked the fact that this was only because two glaring errors in the Report cancelled each other out. Sir Robert Kane's criticism in 1885 that the railways in the interior ran mostly east-west instead of north-south is patent nonsense. The natural course of traffic was east-west; it would have been absurd to try to redirect it.

Secondly, critics claimed that there were too many companies – no fewer than 46 by 1914, and far too many directors – about 300. There should obviously have been much more rapid amalgamation, but this could not work wonders. It could lead to some improvements in efficiency and convenience, but that was all. In fact complaints became even louder as management became somewhat more unified after 1875. The widespread belief that directors' fees swallowed up receipts and led to higher rates was advanced almost annually in parliament by nationalist M. Ps. as grounds for nationalisation or at least amalgamation. This insistence reflects the poverty of much thinking on railway matters, for, while there were too many directors, directorial fees totalled less than £20,000 compared with gross receipts of £4,000,000. For the student of public opinion concerning economic matters it is disconcerting that so much emphasis should have been laid on this irrelevant side issue.

Much more important was the criticism that Irish rates were too high, and that by granting cheaper through-rates to imports than to Irish producers the railways destroyed local industry. Rates were about 30 per cent higher in Ireland than in England in 1900, but this was mainly due to circumstances outside the railways' control. The same basic geographical problems faced the companies before 1914 as face CIE today. A country with a low standard of living, with a falling population, with its industrial centres situated on the coast, with no international through traffic of the type enjoyed by many European countries, with little mineral wealth, offered few opportunities for a policy of bold rate reductions. Geography and demography combined to severely limit the range of rates open to railway managers. To take the most obvious of these factors, mineral traffic before 1914 accounted for nearly 50 per cent of receipts in England and Scotland, but only 15 per cent in Ireland. What this meant in operating terms was spelt out by J. W. Murland, chairman of the Great Northern, when traders complained that rates for coal were higher in Ireland than in England: 'in England coal is carried in train loads for long distances, very often in trucks or wagons belonging to the coal owners; these wagons are put upon the sidings, and consequently the railway company have nothing to do but to haul them to their destinations and there put them upon another siding. In Ireland, on the contrary, we have to carry trucks of coal to various stations; we never have a train load. We carry the coal in our own wagons, for short distances and in such small quantities that they have to be mixed up with other goods; consequently there is a great deal of shunting and marshalling to be done...' The conditions in the two countries were so different that it was quite misleading to simply compare the rates and claim that Irish railways must be inefficient because their charges were higher. To take another example, the rate for artificial manure from Dublin to Longford was 10s. 7d. for one ton, 6s. 5d. a ton for a consignment of six tons; Irish farmers rarely combined to purchase six tons, and consequently paid the higher charge; the English farmer bought in bulk, and paid the lower rate. Butter merchants were particularly vociferous critics of the railways, alleging that Danish lines provided special butter vans so that Danish butter arrived fresh and clean in England, while Irish butter was damaged in transit by careless handling and by lack of special wagons.

But Danish farmers supplied butter all the year round, Irish farmers for only six months, and it was not altogether reasonable to expect the railways to build special vans to lie idle for half the year. The Great Southern & Western did eventually introduce special wagons in 1903 but had to withdraw them within a year because of the irregular supply. Responsibility for the unsatisfactory condition of the butter trade in the late nineteenth century certainly did not lie solely with the railways.

Through rates for imports were lower than local rates. This was standard international practice, and in England traders were making precisely the same complaints against English companies giving preferential rates to imports from America. The 'preferential rates' controversy obscures the real issues affecting the decline of local industry. The railway did kill many local firms in rural Ireland, not through preferential rates but simply by the natural reduction in transport costs. The three most important industries in the interior of the country in 1850 were brewing, distilling and milling. All three were seriously affected in the next thirty years. Local industry, no longer protected by high transport costs from the competition of larger and more efficient producers, was frequently doomed. Paradoxically it was killed, not by poverty but by prosperity, as the local market became sufficiently large to tempt Dublin and English manufacturers. And this was the problem. Would English or Dublin businessmen capture the new market – that was the kernel of the preferential rates question, not the survival of local industry as such. Rural industry was killed as much by Dublin, as by English competition. Because all lines led to Dublin, because Dublin was the centre of the railway system, other coastal towns declined in relative importance after 1850. We know of the spectacular growth of Belfast in the nineteenth century. Dublin's growth was less spectacular, but of even more pervasive influence, and it was the railway, extending its tentacles, octopus-like, north, south and west that allowed Dublin achieve a dominance over the economy (outside the north-east) by 1914 undreamt of a century earlier.

The railway made an important contribution to the increase in the flow of money incomes in the economy after 1850, as even its most vehement critics admitted, like the Corkman we quoted earlier, who agreed that 'bad as this Bandon line has been, it has nonetheless been of incalculable benefit to the district'. It is noteworthy that when asked to prescribe for the plight of the Congested Districts, most railway critics could only answer 'build more railways', advice which was heeded, with lines like the Killorglin & Valentia being opened in 1893, the Westport & Mallaranny in 1894 and the Galway & Clifden in 1895. Some of the complaints against the companies were legitimate, but railway managers had little difficulty in refuting most of the specific charges brought against them by irate traders. After 1873 competition became especially keen as English manufacturers, facing depression and falling profit margins at home, attempted to capture a larger share of the Irish market, and the railway offered a convenient scapegoat for the incompetent or just unlucky native trader unable to sell his own uncompetitive goods. In depression, as always, protectionist and nationalist sentiment revived in some trading sectors, particularly as the deepest phase of the depression in the 1880's coincided with the centenary of Grattan's Parliament, at that time wrongly believed to have conferred unprecedented economic benefits on the country; and nationalisation of the railways was a popular plank in the nationalist economic platform.

The railway age ends in 1914. The problems created by the steep rise in labour costs during the first world war, and by the coming of the motor car and the lorry, proved insoluble. But the change from rail back to road was less dramatic and of less fundamental economic significance than the change eighty years previously from road or water to rail. Before 1845 the transport system was grossly inadequate to the country's needs. 600 miles of inland waterway were then in use. Now 1,000 miles of railway were built in a decade. The impact was profound. In 1845 goods traffic from Galway took four or five days to reach Dublin, in 1851 only ten hours. Galway was as close to Dublin in 1851 as Maynooth had been six years earlier. Before 1850 economic development had been hindered by an underdeveloped transport network. Since 1850 Ireland has been an underdeveloped economy with a highly developed transport system.

INDUSTRIAL DECLINE IN THE NINETEENTH CENTURY

BY

E. R. R. Green

We must begin, I think, by taking a look at the actual terms of the Act of Union before discussing any aspect of Irish industrial history in the nineteenth century. By so doing, we shall of course learn the conditions under which Ireland became part of the United Kingdom, but we can also find out what is just as important, the assumptions made about the Irish economy and its potential by those in control of policy. The accuracy or otherwise of the assessment need not concern us now; that can be dealt with later on.

The Union, as we well know, was pushed through for reasons of security. The government of the day, faced with an external and even an internal threat from revolutionary France, was convinced that the continued existence of two parliaments could only lead to disaster. Full equality within the United Kingdom was offered in return for the sacrifice of the Irish parliament. It seemed a workable solution. Once Irish Catholics had become a permanent minority in a larger unit the practical objection to giving them equal political rights would have gone. In the event, Catholic emancipation was not so easily achieved, but that is another story. It was also expected that free access to British and Imperial markets would bring such prosperity to Ireland that any nostalgia for the old parliament would soon disappear.

The lack of any serious opposition to the Union on economic grounds is remarkable evidence of the change in ideas which had taken place in the later years of the eighteenth century. The old British Empire had been a business concern which professed to exist only for the profit of Englishmen. A sense of reciprocal advantage had now begun to replace the belief that one country could only prosper at the expense of another. The younger Pitt and his colleagues no longer viewed Ireland as a dangerous competitor. On the contrary, they regarded the creation of a free-trading area for the whole British Isles as a positive gain. It is this aspect of the Union – the idea of a common market – which makes the subject such a fascinating one.

Now, to turn to the provisions of the Act of Union. Matters of trade were covered by the Sixth Article which began with a declaratory clause guaranteeing equality of treatment to Ireland. This meant that Ireland was now free to participate in the hitherto jealously guarded colonial trade. In future, she would be automatically included in all trade treaties signed with foreign countries. Irish linen, for instance, would qualify for a bounty on export under this clause just as if it had been made in England or Scotland.

In principle, trade between Great Britain and Ireland was to be completely free – 'all articles, the growth, produce, or manufacture of either country, shall from henceforth be imported into each country from the other, free from duty.' As Lord Castlereagh had noted on a draft of the commercial article, the ideal was 'that the counties of Ireland should be like so many English counties, and goods pass from the one to the other without interruption.' In practice, it was recognised that existing barriers could not disappear overnight. For one thing, so long as Ireland retained a separate exchequer it was necessary to reconcile the taxation systems by the imposition of countervailing duties.

Of more interest to us just now was the problem of what to do about those Irish industries which enjoyed tariff protection against English competitors. The sponsors of the Union were not particularly friendly to the claims of the Irish manufacturers for continued protection, arguing correctly enough that the end result was higher prices to the consumer. It was recognised, though, that the industries concerned were in some cases of recent growth and that capital had been invested in them in expectation of protection. A compromise was accordingly arrived at which provided for a ten per cent *ad valorem* duty on some eighteen articles until 1821. The contention was that any industry which required a higher level of protection did not deserve to survive. The favoured industries produced a range of consumer goods such as silk, leather, glass, hardware and furniture.

The woollen industry was something of a test case if only because of the ruthlessness with which it had been treated by England a century before. It was now provided that protection for Irish woollen manufactures should continue at the existing ate for the full twenty years, although duty at the same level was to be imposed on these goods if they were exported to England. On the Irish side, the concession of free export of wool from England was regarded as even stronger evidence of good intent. Castlereagh's comments in this connection are interesting:

This gives more means than she ever had of being a woollen country. England gives her this without recalling any of her protection given to her linens. Here Ireland has not one trade secured on a supposed compact of giving up another, but both secured to her for ever. It being indifferent where the wealth settles, so it is within a United Kingdom.

Calicoes and muslins secured the most preferential treatment of the lot, duties being maintained at the existing level until

1808 and then reduced progressively until they reached ten per cent in 1816. Cotton yarn and twist were treated similarly except that in their case protection was to cease completely in 1816. The young Irish cotton industry had, in fact, succeeded rather well in its plea for consideration as a special case.

These are the main provisions of the Act of Union with which we need be concerned. It is important to know them because the possibility has to be considered that there were political causes and remedies for the troubles which beset the Irish economy in the century that followed. There are other factors which have not so far been discussed such as the limited natural resources of the country, the defects of its social structure, and the inevitably close relationship to the British economy. We shall have an opportunity to observe their influence as we now go on to trace the outlines of the industrial history of Ireland during the last century.

The return of peace in 1815 also unfortunately proved the end of a remarkable period of economic growth in Ireland which had lasted for about fifty years. The postwar recession was over by 1819, but the Irish economy remained stagnant. As growth slowed down, the flaws in the economic and social structure began to appear. Rents bore heavily on the farmers who now had to be content with much lower prices for their produce. Population continued to grow even though the economy had ceased to expand and there was a sharp increase in unemployment and poverty in consequence. The headlong pace of development in England was rapidly concentrating industry in areas where coal and iron ore were available and with ready access to markets. Industrial undertakings in less favoured regions such as Ireland became uncompetitive and sooner or later went to the wall. The development of an efficient transport system based on steam navigation and railways further strengthened the ascendancy of the great industrial districts.

The operation of these natural forces makes the actions of ministers and parliaments seem somewhat puny by comparison, but they were not without effect. Irish difficulties, for instance, were undoubtedly intensified by monetary policy. By 1821 both Great Britain and Ireland had returned to gold and in 1826 the two currencies were amalgamated. This entailed a severe deflation which was an important cause of economic depression in Ireland. Some modern scholars, indeed, have argued that deflation rather than the Union was the cause of Irish misery. I think, though, that such a view tends to underestimate the fundamental seriousness of the Irish situation. In any case, the Union and the maintenance of a par with sterling were very much aspects of the same thing.

There was also the matter of the Union duties which came up for consideration in 1820. The government first decided to continue them at ten per cent until 1825 and to postpone their final abolition until 1840. The reaction showed the extent to which the hesitant liberalism of 1800 had hardened into free trade dogma within twenty years. The Manchester Chamber of Commerce, which had been recently founded but whose word was soon to become law in such matters, led a chorus of protest with the complaint that 'to levy duties on merchandise passing between parts of the same Empire is injurious to their common prosperity and contrary to the just principles of political economy.' A commission of inquiry was then appointed by the government which agreed that the Union duties were 'wholly incompatible with that state of entire union and unrestrained intercourse.' It was recommended that they should be abolished by 1829. The Tory free traders in the government were not prepared to delay even that long and a clear sweep of all surviving duties was made in 1824.

The repeal of the Union duties followed by the economic crisis of 1826 marks the stage at which Union became integration. This meant that the Irish economy was now forced back onto those kinds of activity for which it was endowed by nature or in which it had developed some special skill. There was precious little of the latter other than the linen industry. It was a matter, then, of concentrating on the production of foodstuffs to satisfy the English market. In return, English manufactured goods of better quality and lower cost than could possibly have been produced in Ireland were imported. In the abstract this all seemed very sensible and was the way in which well-informed Englishmen viewed the situation, but the social costs were high.

I propose then, to say something of the consequences of the rapid industrial decay which followed the repeal of the Union duties and which it is important to remember might well have been inevitable in any case. The reduction of transport costs with the coming of cross-channel steamer services and the development of the railway system would have made it increasingly difficult to protect small Irish industries whose only base was the domestic market. There is poignant evidence of what took place in the pages of the bulky reports of royal commissions and select committees which were appointed year in and year out to inquire into Irish conditions. Governments which were inhibited from action by the economic orthodoxy of the day seem to have been all the more avid for information.

A town like Drogheda was an excellent example of industrial decline. It had been perhaps the most important textile centre outside the north of Ireland, but within a dozen years the number of handloom weavers fell to a third or a quarter even of their former strength. By 1840 there were under two thousand of them, over half earning no more than 4s. to 6s. a week. They eked out a living by begging, collecting manure, and taking land in conacre to grow potatoes. The rise of flax-spinning by power had made it difficult for domestic weavers to get supplies of yarn. Cotton weavers had been pushed out by the spread of the powerloom in England. The more fortunate, as we must no doubt regard them, had gone to Lancashire or the Scottish linen-making area around Dundee.

Bandon, although a smaller place, suffered even more complete disaster. Up to 1829 the town had between 1,500 and 2,000 handloom weavers, but ten years later there were no more than 150. There were supposed to be 1,500 of them in Manchester and as many more again in London. As the commissioners who inquired into the condition of the poorer classes in Ireland in 1836 said in their report, what had happened was 'attributable to the vain endeavour to maintain a competition by handlooms against mechanical power.'

Cork lost its textile industries like other southern towns; it was alleged in 1836 that the weavers had mostly gone off to Manchester. More serious by far was the decline of the great provision trade. In the eighteenth century when the export of live cattle from Ireland to England was forbidden in any case, a ready demand developed for salt beef, pork, and butter to the sugar plantations of the West Indies and the Newfoundland fishery and for victualling the army, navy and merchant marine. Cork was the chief centre, but within twenty years after the peace of 1815 the trade had shrunk to a quarter of its former size. First, there came the reduction in demand for the armed forces. Then followed the opening of the colonial trade in 1825 and the loss of the North American market to the United States. Finally, after the introduction of the cross-channel steamers cattle were no longer slaughtered in Ireland but shipped to England as stores.

Eighteenth-century Dublin had been the second city of the Empire and a number of industries had developed there to satisfy an upper-class demand for such things as silk, glassware, books, furniture and coaches. Postwar deflation probably hurt these trades more than the Union, although it cannot have helped, but improved transport was no doubt the decisive factor in their decay by subjecting them to intensive competition from across the water. The silk industry was a conspicuous victim, losing protection in 1824, and declining rapidly until there were only some 400 weavers left about fifteen years later. Many of the workers settled in the English silk-manufacturing town of Macclesfield. It is interesting to note that poplin was able to survive because it was a distinctive product not easily available elsewhere.

Dublin tradesmen had enjoyed high wages because skill was scarce in the agricultural economy of Ireland and the city had a dominant market position. The men fought hard to maintain their wage levels. Robert Hutton, the coachmaker, claimed before a select committee in 1824 that the wages of skilled labour in Dublin were as high as in London while the cost of living was twenty-five per cent lower. Contemporary opinion tended to see this as particularly reprehensible and accordingly to lay the blame for the decline of Dublin industries on the trade unions. The very considerable power of the unions in the city was undoubtedly a cause of rigidity in industry, but it is doubtful if it could have been saved simply by lowering wages.

Against this picture of industrial decay in the towns of the South must be set the rise of Belfast as a thriving industrial town. While we are not concerned in this talk with the emergence of a regional economy in Ulster it cannot altogether be ignored. It was analogous to the shift of the economic centre of gravity in England from the South and West to the Midlands and North. Easy access to the Clyde and Mersey were contributing factors as well as the more favourable social structure of Ulster. In the last analysis though, it was the presence of the linen industry which ensured the province a different future from the rest of Ireland. A successful transition to flax-spinning by power was carried through in the 'thirties of the last century which ensured its survival over the rival industries of Leeds and Dundee. The reorganisation of the linen industry meant a serious loss of income to farm families where the women had spun on the wheel and the men wove on the loom. The industry was now concentrated in Belfast to a great extent and almost disappeared outside the province of Ulster.

In a brief sketch such as this it would plainly be impossible to trace Irish industrial history in detail right through the century. The period of greatest interest in any case is that which follows the repeal of the Union duties and when improved transport methods created a single market economy for the whole United Kingdom. As a matter of fact, little interest was shown in the industrial sector of the economy until after 1880. By then the years of agricultural prosperity which followed the Great Famine had come to an end and intense competition from abroad had shown up the deficiencies of farming practice in Ireland. It was not only British agriculture which suffered from foreign competition, but industry was also becoming sharply aware of thrusting rivals in overseas markets. The changing position of Britain in international trade brought a corresponding weakening of the authority of free trade dogma. Undoubtedly it was this as much as anything else which led to interest in industrial development in Ireland.

The report of the select committee of 1885 on industries in Ireland really marks the beginning of industrial revival if only by drawing attention to a truly alarming state of affairs. Irishmen had become more or less reconciled to the loss of handicrafts and the disappearance of local breweries, tanneries, rope-walks and the like, but now the basic agricultural life of the country and the trades dependent upon it were also threatened.

The fate of the milling industry was a good example of what had happened. Despite reduced acreages of grain and shrinking population, the industry had maintained its ground and had a useful export market in England. Then the competition of American flour, milled from wheat grown on the virgin prairie and ground in modern plant using the improved roller system, put two-thirds of the Irish mills out of business within ten years. In time, the tide was turned by rising home demand in America, by the introduction of rollers, and by the use of Canadian and South American wheat which produced better flour. The milling industry was also stimulated by the increasing use of imported maize for livestock feeding.

The dairying industry, too, was caught between the competition of superior butter from Denmark and elsewhere and a cheap substitute in the form of margarine, or butterine as it was then called. The butter trade also suffered, as did the millers, from low through-rates on steamers and railways which enabled Dutch butterine, for instance, to be sent to Dublin at lower cost than butter from Cork. To survive, it became essential, as Sir Horace Plunkett said, to 'change from a home to a factory industry.' Under his influence, the new creameries developed to a large extent on a co-operative basis, to replace farmhouse butter by creamery butter.

A less well-known example of industrial revival was the woollen industry which was able to create a market on the basis of distinctive products such as tweed and frieze. The use of the trade name 'ulster' for a particular type of frieze overcoat from about 1879 is one evidence of success. An early mill was that at Kilmacthomas in which Lord Waterford took an active interest, although the Athlone mills, opened in 1859, were perhaps the more successful.

It is now time to sum up. Rapid economic development in the eighteenth century combined with the protection given by primitive transport conditions had enabled the country to achieve a modest growth of industry. In Ulster, this was adequate foundation for a regional economy with a sizeable industrial sector. Elsewhere in the country, industry proved too feeble to long withstand English rivals once transport costs were appreciably lowered.

The pathetic fallacy of the Union was a belief that conditions of equality were all that Ireland needed to prosper. In fact, it can only have hastened the appearance of a serious regional imbalance not only in the British Isles but within Ireland as well. Modern policy of course would have attempted to stimulate industry, but the historian must always feel uneasy about blaming men in the past for not taking action considered appropriate in his own time. In any case, it is very doubtful if Irish economic problems could have been satisfactorily settled by any government, the unemployment problem created by a rapidly growing population alone was so very serious.

The real failure of nineteenth-century Ireland, it seems to me, was not with wool or cotton or glass, but in leather, meat-packing, fish-curing, cheese, farm machinery. This comes out strongly in the first Census of Production in 1907. The most important group of industries in Ireland were those concerned with food and drink, with a total output of over £27 million in value, nearly twice that of textiles, the next most important group. Brewing and distilling, grain-milling, and bacon and butter, taken together, were all of about equal importance. Ireland produced nearly two-thirds of the butter made in the United Kingdom, over a third of the bacon and a quarter of the spirits.

It was in an industry like tanning that performance was notably weak – a mere £87,000 worth out of a United Kingdom total of £18 million – where the raw material might have been readily available. Only £6,000 worth of cheese was produced in Ireland in that year. The milling industry produced over half the United Kingdom output of maize meal, but on the other hand requirements of agricultural implements and fertilizer were to a large extent imported ready for use. The conspicuous though isolated success of Guinness's brewery shows that success might just have been possible. It would be incautious, I think, to go any further in suggesting that industrial decay was not to a large extent inevitable.

VIII

THE INDUSTRIALISATION OF THE NORTH-EAST

BY

J. M. Goldstrom

At the beginning of the nineteenth century Irishmen were optimistic about the economic future of their country. It looked as though Ireland was on the verge of an industrial revolution. The conditions seemed promising. Irish farmers were producing more and more cereals, meat and dairy produce, for which they were getting extremely good prices. Landlords and tenants alike, throughout the country, were enjoying a higher standard of living and all social classes but the poorest could afford consumer goods that had previously been beyond reach. The demand for these goods was opening up opportunities for commerce and industry, and there was no lack of labour to man the workshops, factories, warehouses and shops, because Ireland's population was rising rapidly. There was no shortage of foreign exchange to bring raw materials and machinery into the country, because the export trade was booming. Nor was there any shortage of capital, for the linen manufacturers, merchants, landlords, even some of the farming community of the country, were accumulating savings.

Geographically, the country was well endowed. There were good harbours, plenty of fast-flowing streams for water power, and good roads. Her people were not lacking in intelligence or enterprise, and so far as education was concerned, though their schools were few enough, they were nevertheless more numerous than in England. Finally, the country had.

prior to 1800, a government which did its best to encourage home industry. It had helped to keep foreign goods out, by placing heavy duties on imports, and it had encouraged industrial development with cash grants.

We know, now, that the only part of Ireland to become fully industrialised was Belfast and the surrounding area. The reasons for Belfast's development are not hard to find. The area had abundant water power and a good harbour. It was, moreover, linked with the rest of Ulster by the Lagan Valley. This valley provided a communicating corridor with other parts of Ulster for the collection of homespun linen yarn and linen web. Belfast had grown sizeably in the eighteenth century and benefited more than any other town in Ireland from the expansion of linen manufacturing, so when cotton manufacturing was introduced to Ireland in the 1770's it soon gravitated to Belfast, because many of the techniques required for its marketing and production were established features of the linen industry. Furthermore, Belfast was blessed with enterprising businessmen, who realised the advantages of the modern methods of spinning cotton by machine that were being pioneered in Lancashire, and as early as 1784 a water-powered spinning mill was constructed outside Belfast, the first of its kind in Ireland. The industry was fortunate. It obtained cash grants from the Irish Linen Board and the government cushioned it from foreign competition by placing high tariffs on imported cotton. Not surprisingly, growth was rapid. In the Belfast region in 1790 there were 8,000 people employed in cotton spinning. Twenty years later the number had trebled. And that is not taking into account the thousands such as weavers, textile printers, mechanics, warehousemen and clerks, who were indirectly employed by the industry. Wages were as high, or higher, than they were in Lancashire; a writer of the time commented that 'a smart young cotton weaver became no slight attraction in the eyes of a country belle.' The need of the industry to import large quantities of coal and cotton tied it to the Belfast area, and iron foundries, calico printing, steam engine manufacturing, general engineering and marketing and banking enterprises developed in the area. Belfast was becoming by far the most prosperous place in Ireland.

Unfortunately, the prosperity of the cotton industry did not last – the industry was swept away by a series of depressions following the Napoleonic wars, and by the middle of the century hardly a trace remained, save for the miserably-paid cottage weavers working for Scottish contractors. There is a traditional explanation for the decline of the industry, which blames the Act of Union that took away Ireland's independence. Protection of cotton was gradually whittled away after the Act, and abolished in 1821, thereby it is said, ruining a promising industry. This argument may be soothing to national pride, but it is unsound. The real difficulty was that the market for cotton goods was not large enough to guarantee the industry's future. In particular after the Napoleonic wars agricultural prices fell sharply, and Irishmen had less money to spend on consumer goods such as sheets, dresses and shirts. If the industry had been export-based, it could have taken advantage of the ravenous overseas market for cheap machine-spun cotton. Instead, cushioned against outside competition, the industry had been producing inferior goods, inefficiently, at high cost. Supposing the tariff barriers had been retained indefinitely after the Act of Union, the Irish manufacturers could not have kept pace with their highly efficient Lancashire rivals, who were constantly cutting down on their costs and selling more cheaply. Sooner or later the point would have been reached when no tariff barriers could have kept English cotton out of the Irish market.

During the cotton boom the Ulster linen industry declined

in relative importance, especially in the Belfast area, where it lost workers to the cotton industry. Cottage weavers who lived within a day's walking distance of a cotton mill found it paid better to collect machine-spun cotton yarn and weave it at home than to weave home-spun linen yarn. In addition to losing workers, the linen industry was suffering at the hands of its foreign rivals who were developing machinery for spinning yarn. In 1788 a machine had been developed that could spin coarse cotton yarn, and the Scottish and English manufacturers who took it up were fast putting the Irish coarse yarn producers out of business. In 1825 a further refinement in the industry made it possible for fine linen yarn, too, to be spun by machine. However, on this occasion the Irish manufacturers rallied – they stood to lose heavily if they didn't. The bleach greens of the Lagan and Bann valleys represented a great deal of capital, and the north-east had idle cotton mills, skilled labour and supplies of locally-grown flax. The new machines were installed in and around Belfast and one of the first of the linen mills was an old cotton-spinning factory, rebuilt in 1828 after it had burned down. The linen industry had found its old vigour again, and since it exploited export markets to the full it was not hampered by lack of home demand. In twenty years there were more linen spindles in Ireland than in England or in Scotland, and the population of Belfast, now depending heavily on the industry for employment, doubled within these years.

Although linen was now spun by machine it was still being woven by hand in cottages throughout Ulster. It was not until after the Famine that power-loom weaving made its appearance in Ireland. The Famine had depleted the country's labour force and weavers were relatively scarce, and consequently able to command high rates. Employers in the linen industry began to investigate the possibilities of machine weaving, and found the method cheaper and more efficient. Gradually, the provincial handloom weavers were supplanted by factory operatives around Belfast. By 1860 some 4,000 power looms were operating in the country, most of them in the north-east. The American civil war of 1861-5 had one fortunate effect on the industry – the disruption of cotton supplies from the American south led to a world shortage, and linen was in demand as a substitute. By the end of the war there were four times as many power looms in Ireland.

In the middle of the century Belfast acquired its second major industry, iron shipbuilding. Shipbuilding was not, of course, new to Belfast, and records of launchings go back to the seventeenth century. William Ritchie's shipyard, established in 1791, was still functioning, but as long as ships were made from timber, operations were bound to remain on a small scale. It was difficult to compete with American and Canadian shipbuilders, who had unlimited cheap timber to build with. But the situation changed completely once it was cheaper to build ships from iron. Belfast was ideal. It had the essential combination of spacious land and deep water, whereas across the Channel the Merseyside shipbuilders were in trouble. They were being crowded out by the expansion of the Liverpool docks. The Belfast Harbour Commissioners were very anxious to attract shipbuilding and repairing to the city and had the foresight to engage in extensive alterations to the harbour. They straightened the channel of the Lagan, forming in the process a large piece of land, now known as Queen's Island, on which they built a patent slip and a timber pond. Sites were offered at low rents to constructors and repairers. It so happened that in 1851 the Belfast iron-works was opened, with great fanfare, patriotically making iron plates from Irish coal and ore. It hadn't a chance of competing with English imports, and closed down in a few years. The proprietor, William Hickson, left high and dry with countless iron plates to dispose of, hit upon the idea of turning them into ships, and took a lease on Queen's Island. He was soon floundering in the complex problems of shipbuilding and in 1854 advertised for an experienced manager to extricate him. By one of the more fortunate accidents of history, an accident that was to turn Belfast into one of the world's foremost centres of shipbuilding, the man who answered the advertisement was Edward Harland, an Englishman who had served an apprenticeship under the great Robert Stephenson. Harland reorganised the yard, bought Hickson out within four years, and took as his partner G. W. Wolff, a Liverpool engineer of German origin.

Harland was the technical genius of the partnership. Until his time the design of iron ships had scarcely differed from timber vessels. But Harland had an engineer's understanding of the possibilities of the new material, and built his ships roughly in the shape of a box girder. They were very long and narrow, with iron decks and fairly flat bottoms. They were immensely strong and seaworthy, had more cargo and passenger space than conventional ships, and were economical with fuel. His rivals called them floating coffins, and predicted they would break in two. In fact, they turned out to be so good that customers took to sending back their purchases to Belfast to have them further lengthened.

Wolff obtained the orders for the firm. He was related to one of the owners of the Liverpool-based Bibby Line, and most of the ocean-going ships built in the first ten years were commissioned by them. Wolff proceeded to establish an even more important connection with the giant White Star Line, and the firm built more than fifty steamers for them over the next forty years. The first White Star liner, the *Oceanic*, launched in 1870, was in its day the fastest and most luxurious Atlantic liner afloat. The company's reputation for advanced design and high quality earned them orders for large liners and much-prized prestige contracts for the Navy. This reputation filled their order book and made it possible for Harland and Wolff to escape the recessions that plagued their rivals. They expanded steadily. Between 1870 and 1910 their labour force increased fivefold. In 1910 they were launching the gigantic *Olympic*, and had the ill-fated *Titanic* on the stocks. In 1879 another large shipyard had been established on Queen's Island by Workman, Clark and Co., building rather smaller vessels. The two yards ranked among the giants of British shipbuilding – in the first decade of the twentieth century the Harland and Workman firms were, respectively, the second and fourth-largest ship-builders in terms of tonnage built. Between them they built about a quarter of the total United Kingdom tonnage.

Linen and shipbuilding were the dominant industries of the north-east – linen was the larger, if we judge by the total number of people employed, shipbuilding was larger if we judge by the employment it afforded in Belfast. But Belfast had many other industries, too, most of them springing up to meet the needs of these two giants. Spinning machines, scutching and hackling equipment were made in the city. So were steam engines, foundry products, ropes, and heating and ventilating equipment. Manufacturers diversified and produced tea-drying equipment, stable fittings, agricultural machinery, motor cars, mineral waters and cigarettes. Much of the output found its way to Britain or went abroad.

Before the first world war began Belfast had a population approaching 400,000 and it was one of the prosperous cities of the British Isles. Wages had kept pace with those in British cities, and there was little unemployment. Workers in fact were better off than in most industrial cities because the linen industry gave employment to their womenfolk. However, the inhabitants paid a heavy price. They lived in rows of mean, hastily-built houses, over-hung by a constant pall of industrial smoke, and they worked long hours in factories that were dangerous and unhealthy. Even so, we should bear in mind that conditions in Belfast were not as squalid as they were in many British cities. Belfast had built its industrial housing estates later than Manchester and Birmingham, for example. One of the less happy consequences of Belfast's rapid expansion was the competition that developed between Catholics and Protestants coming to the city for work and housing – a competition that bred animosity, and eventually riots, and led to the present situation of rigidly demarcated Catholic and Protestant zones that has earned for Belfast its unenviable reputation for religious intolerance.

If we look beyond Belfast and its surrounding towns to the other parts of Ulster, there was little development in the nineteenth century. Londonderry processed tobacco, built a few ships, and was the focus of a shirt-making industry, and scattered through the province were a few spinning mills, distilleries and flour mills. But during this period Ulster's rural industries contracted. Even in the area around Londonderry the employment that shirt manufacturers provided for outworkers was small compensation for the loss of domestic weaving and spinning. As rural industries declined, ambitious men moved to Belfast or emigrated. The Ulster that lay beyond Belfast had more in common with the rest of Ireland than it had with its principal city.

The key to the prosperity of the north-east was its dependence on foreign markets. Even in the eighteenth century the linen industry relied on the English market, and foreign markets became absolutely vital in the nineteenth century. This helps to explain why, in the nineteenth century, Ulstermen were determined to keep close links with England, when the rest of the country was demanding self-government in the hope that it would, amongst other things, stimulate home industries. But Belfast's reliance on foreign markets left the linen industry in particular exposed to fluctuations in world trade, and from time to time there were severe depressions. Looking back now, we can say with hindsight that the linen industry's long-term prospects were uncertain. It was not growing as fast as in the eighteenth century, in spite of the fact that it was helped along by the decline of Scottish and English rivals from the mid-nineteenth century. Their misfortunes provided more customers for the Irish manufacturers, and the industry continued to grow. But it was now growing faster than world demand, and eventually the Ulster producers found themselves with excess capacity.

During the first world war the north-east enjoyed boom conditions. The demand for ships was enormous, and linen was in demand for aeroplane canvas. The boom continued intermittently after the war, but in the mid 'twenties severe depression set in. There was a reduction in international trade, which worsened as country after country imposed restrictions on imports. As so large a proportion of Ulster's products was exported, the region was hit very hard. In 1930 there were thousands of unemployed linen workers, in 1933 Harland and Wolff failed to launch a single ship and in 1934 Workman and Clark went out of business. One of the saddest sights of these times was to see grass growing on the slipyards. Between the wars only Wales rivalled Northern Ireland's unemployment rate within the United Kingdom, and in the worst years one man in four was unemployed.

Linen and shipbuilding had a reprieve during the second world war but both are declining now, and their future is bleak. Fortunately their place is being taken by a variety of engineering, electrical and textile undertakings which have been attracted to the region from the over-crowded and labour-starved midlands and home counties of England by grants and cheap factory sites. Northern Ireland as a whole has the highest unemployment rate in the United Kingdom and the lowest average earnings, but prosperity has come back to Belfast.

I suggested at the beginning of this talk that at the start of the nineteenth century Ireland seemed ripe for industrial revolution. Why is it that the industrial development of which Belfast was the centre failed to spread through the country? Little research has been undertaken on this subject, but it is a very important question, and I would like here to make some tentative suggestions. The most important prerequisite for Ireland if she was to industrialise was a thriving agricultural sector. Farmers needed to produce enough food for people in the town and in the country areas, leaving a surplus for export. The farmers' income had to be enough for them to buy the agricultural equipment they needed, and also to buy consumer goods. Only thus would there be stimulus for new industries. Furthermore, farmers ought to have made enough profits to be able to save, so that their savings could be channelled into industrial investment. Certainly the farmers were coping with the first task, for year after year production of grain and livestock rose, and exports soared. But the profits were small, so demand for manufactured products was not buoyant. In pre-famine Ireland the profits were small because output was raised by employing more labour, rather than by modernising methods and equipment. This meant that the land had to provide a living for too many people. From 1815 agricultural prices fell, landlords got less rent, and a great many of the swelling population had barely enough to eat. Obviously, in these conditions, people had less money than ever for manufactured goods. There were people in Ireland with capital to invest, but who was going to invest in industries, if the market was limited, and if what market there was had to be shared with rising imports from Britain?

It was only in the north-east that industries took root, but it is a sad fact that these were not of the kind to encourage growth in the rest of Ireland. The most suitable industry for a developing economy is one that helps to stimulate others. Ideally, it requires a good range of locally-produced raw materials and equipment for the stimulation of further industries, these in turn expanding so as to stimulate more. Ideally, the product of the first industry should entail further manufacturing stages before it reaches the consumer. In short, the best possible industry for a developing economy is an initial enterprise that is capable of setting off a chain reaction of industrial activity.

As I have said, the industries of the north-east were not of this kind. The cotton industry imported its raw materials from abroad, which could only help the import merchants and, perhaps, shipping business. Irish coal turned out to be of poor quality and expensive to mine, so native mining did not prosper. Cotton producers needed spinning machines and steam engines, but not very many, and much of the machinery was built out of wood in the mills themselves. Those industries that cotton had brought into existence never became large enough to make a significant impact on the economy, with the single exception of engineering. Cotton was able to give employment to handloom weavers, but that was a cottage industry with no future. Cotton was instrumental in the development of Belfast, and provided the basis for a revitalised linen industry, but it fell short of starting an Irish industrial revolution.

The linen industry had somewhat more impact in the Belfast region, though little on the country as a whole. True, it bought Irish flax, a useful source of income for many farmers, but in later years foreign flax was cheaper and better, and local flax-growing declined in the last quarter of the nineteenth century. The linen industry had provided employment for the handloom weavers of Ulster, but that disappeared with mechanisation of weaving. The only service that the giant shipbuilding industry performed for the country as a whole was to offer employment in Belfast as an alternative to emigration. Virtually all the ships were for export and most of the industry's requirements were imported or produced in Belfast. In other words, the north-east was never an integral part of the Irish economy.

Had Ireland been able to develop a wider range of industries, a range perhaps involving a greater degree of processing of agricultural products, the outcome might have been happier. Unfortunately, Ireland was too close to the English food markets, and once steam ships arrived in the 1820's it became more profitable to concentrate on the exporting of live cattle, pigs and sheep. This made good economic sense to Irish farmers but it did mean that Ireland became a pastoral country. The craving for land may have accentuated this trend. The rural Irishman prized land above all, and the more so because by the early nineteenth century security of tenure was imperilled by growing competition for land. It was his instinct, where he had security of tenure, and the modest prosperity that came with it, to skimp and scrape to acquire more. After the Famine holdings were consolidated, and the result of this was a drastic reduction in the small-holdings and plots once so numerous. This close attachment to the land by those working it has cost Ireland many of her ablest young men. They emigrated to London, Liverpool, Boston or New York because there was no land for them to inherit, or because they were not prepared to wait for it until they were middle-aged. In recent years industrialisation of the south of Ireland has grown apace, and there are signs that she may perhaps rival the north-east in the long run. The economic history of Ireland since 1850 has still to be written, but when it is, perhaps we shall have a clearer view of the processes that have made modern Ireland.

IX

IRISH ECONOMIC HISTORY:
FACT AND MYTH

BY

L. M. Cullen

One of the themes of this series has been that Irish economic development is more independent of non-economic factors than has been generally believed. In particular, political and religious factors were far from having a decisive influence in the economic field. The penal laws, for instance, scarcely account for the underdevelopment of the Irish economy. In the political sphere Grattan's Parliament was not responsible for the economic expansion of the late eighteenth century. One can go even farther. Irish conditions were in many ways akin to those in other agricultural countries or in the agricultural regions of industrialising Britain. Population grew as rapidly or even more rapidly in other countries. Moreover, it is possible that the causes of population growth were common to all these countries. Likewise industrial decline in the nineteenth century in Ireland was paralleled in rural areas elsewhere.

There is, of course, superficially at any rate, a paradox in Irish economic development. The economic growth of the eighteenth century turned into the industrial decline of the nineteenth century. There is no doubt either of the eighteenth-century expansion or of the nineteenth-century reversal. The only question in doubt is the explanation of the reversal. Because decline followed the Union, it was supposed that it was caused by the Union. This necessarily presupposed that economic change and the Union approximately coincided.

This was not in fact true; the correlation between the withdrawal of protection in the first quarter of the century and industrial decline is poor enough. Moreover, much industry in factory and in a domestic setting alike survived into the 1840's and even later. This retardation in decline in the first forty years of the century and acceleration subsequently appear to contradict the thesis that the seeds of economic decline lay in the Act of Union itself. However, O'Connell's agitation for the repeal of the Union identified what was described as the 'commercial injustices' of the Union as the cause of the economic difficulties with which the country had to cope in the nineteenth century. There were, however, no injustices in the commercial clauses of the Act of Union. Moreover, Irish tariffs before the Union were already too low to effectively exclude English manufactures. Of course it could be argued that in the Union Ireland had conceded the right to impose or adjust tariffs. This is perfectly true but it removes the emphasis from tariffs to the right to impose tariffs. Apart from the satisfaction of frustrated political aspirations, the benefits of tariff protection appeared much greater than they were in reality. Moreover, with domestically-organised activity and small-scale factories both finding it difficult to compete with new competition, protection would have all the more failed to offer a solution to the emerging problems of modern Ireland.

The real determinants of Irish economic retardation, although political resentment obscured the issue, lay outside the legislative and, almost equally although perhaps less obviously, outside the fiscal sphere. Externally these determinants were the technological and organisational advances of the Industrial Revolution and the radical improvement in transport wrought by the railways; internally the growth of population. These factors are distinct, although they are of course closely related. On the one hand, technological changes and transport improvements went hand in hand in producing increased competition for small-scale and domestic industry. On the other hand, the undermining of domestic and small industry made the consequences of continued population growth all the more serious. In fact, even if population had ceased to rise in the early decades of the century, it seems certain that at some later stage a serious crisis would have occurred. It is understandable that the adverse implications of the technological changes were underrated at the time, because previously Irish industry had benefited from new forms of technology and organisation. In the case of population growth also contemporaries were led to underrate its role in the growth of poverty because emerging hostility to the landlords as a class sought the causes of poverty in tenurial arrangements and minimised the relevance of economic causes. Short tenures[1], it was argued, encouraged excessive competition and their uncertainty deterred investment. Modern historians, relying on contemporary witnesses, have often tended to seek the causes of population growth in the land system itself. Allegedly discouraging economic betterment, it promoted early marriages through hopelessness, thus leading to the accelerated population growth of the late eighteenth and early nineteenth centuries. But the evidence does not always bear this picture out. For instance, neither subdivision of holdings nor the potato diet, both of which are often considered vital to the process of population growth, were distinctive features of the country at large in the eighteenth century. It is abundantly clear that sub-division of holdings never proceeded very far at all even in the early nineteenth century in a large part of the country,

[1] Leases had become much shorter in the nineteenth century, an accentuation of a trend becoming evident in the late eighteenth century (see p. 15) and powerfully encouraged by price fluctuations in the early nineteenth century.

and the potato diet became widespread only very late and even then with significant social and geographical gradations in the dependence on it.

All this leads to a picture very different from the established one. Indeed, even where historians have come to reject the thesis that political events have shaped Irish economic history, they have often continued to accept the factual picture of poverty and depression itself. This is at first sight surprising. But the fact is that there is a remarkable degree of continuity in the assertions of Irish poverty and depression. A dark picture of eighteenth-century conditions, painted in the polemical writings of the late nineteenth century, appears to be confirmed in contemporary writings of the eighteenth century itself. The apparent strength of this case lies in the continuity of the writings speaking of Irish poverty and depression. But its weakness also lies in this very continuity itself, because it represents an attitude rather than a serious economic appraisal of conditions. What we have to see now is how this attitude was first formed, and how it also came to infuse the historical accounts written in the late nineteenth century of previous Irish history.

The democratic nationalism of the nineteenth century was rather different from that of the eighteenth century. But there were similarities especially in regard to the part Anglo-Irish relations played in political and constitutional issues affecting Ireland, and controversial arguments created in the eighteenth century had a relevance to nineteenth-century political developments. According to a number of eighteenth-century writers, the act in 1699 prohibiting the export of woollens from Ireland had led to general depression. Its notoriety had at first been political. But it easily became economic also as the constitutional ferment of the 1720's made contemporaries prone to find a political cause for the economic difficulties of that decade. The imagined economic consequences of the act were all the more resented because many contemporaries, at a time when trade prospects were poor, felt that the operation of the act deprived the country of one of the few outlets which would have enabled it to pay its external obligations. Some contemporaries argued that the situation would have been very serious indeed but for evasion of the act by smuggling wool and woollen goods abroad. This belief in an extensive smuggling trade was often to be repeated in the course of the eighteenth century. Affirmation however was due almost exclusively to the political appeal of the implication that the act was rendered self-defeating by evasion and that it might therefore be repealed on economic grounds as well as on political grounds. Not all writers of the 1720's had an equally emphatic outlook. Some like Arthur Dobbs, for instance, retained a moderate attitude, although Dobbs himself was much influenced by the arguments abroad about the 1699 act. However, although controversy waned after the 1720's, belief in the arguments put out in that decade never died completely, and in the 1770's they were fitted into a more all-embracing synthesis. The 1770's, like the 1720's, were marked by a coincidence of economic difficulty and political unrest, more acute than they had been for almost fifty years. The American Revolution gave an impetus to the swell of political unrest in Ireland. Economic depression occurred three times within the decade, the last occasion, 1777–1778, coinciding with a sharp rise in political tension. In two works which appeared in 1779 by Sir James Caldwell and John Hely Hutchinson respectively, the interpretation which saw Irish economic development as one determined by a framework of restrictions was most fully worked out. In particular, Hely Hutchinson's work, *The commercial restraints of Ireland,* has, more than any other single work, influenced the interpretation of subsequent historians. Yet Hely Hutchinson's book, or Caldwell's, cannot be regarded as representative of eighteenth-century writing.

Almost as striking as the continuity in Irish attitudes on economic issues are the gaps in this continuity. Attitudes were emphatic in the 1720's and in the late 1770's. But in the intervening years they were noticeably less so. After the late 1770's interest slackened again. The political motivation of much eighteenth-century writing thus seems obvious. This was equally true of writing in the following century. In fact, remarkably little serious study was made of Irish economic issues in the nineteenth century: if parliamentary enquiries are left out of the reckoning, this emerges very clearly. This lack of interest came to be commented on in the late nineteenth century. It was then attributed to the shock caused by the famine. But this is not the reason. Interest in economic issues was at a low ebb even in the decades preceding the Famine.

It was not until the late 1870's that economic development came to the fore again among the issues in Irish life. One reason for this was the revival of interest in repeal of the union, this time in the limited form of home rule. Home rule raised fiscal issues such as the possibility of encouraging Irish industry by tariff protection. But concern with economic development could easily have been as superficial as it had been during the repeal agitation of the 1840's. That it was not so, was due to the sharp industrial depression experienced in the second half of the 1870's. In the early 1840's on the other hand domestic industrial activity still employed a huge number of people, and many small factories still flourished. Domestic industrial activity declined very rapidly from the 1840's, however, and small factories also began to find the competition fiercer. The difficulties came to a head in the 1870's when falling prices and increased outside competition created a threat far more imminent than that hanging over industry in the 1840's. The downward trend of the intervening decades now appeared more obvious, and numerous failures in the 1870's seemed to presage a forthcoming annihilation of industrial activity across much of Ireland. Alarm and the immediacy of the threat led to a quickened interest in industrial matters and to practical efforts to gain support for existing or surviving Irish industries. An industrial exhibition was held in Cork in 1882; one in Dublin in 1883. Dublin Corporation in 1883 appointed a committee to enquire into industrial development and efforts in parliament resulted in the appointment in 1885 of a select committee to enquire into Irish industry.

This resurgence of interest in home rule and in economic development led to an interest in the historical background. This awareness would probably have been as vague as in the 1840's but for the accident of the appearance between 1872 and 1874 of James Anthony Froude's *The English in Ireland*. Froude was no nationalist; a disgruntled English unionist, he was indeed the reverse. But his book had a powerful catalysing effect on Irish historical ideas for two reasons. First, he made known again the economic ideas expressed in the eighteenth century by Swift and Hely Hutchinson. Secondly, he attributed the failure of English rule to misgovernment, a thesis whose appeal to nationalists and home rulers is obvious. Froude was quoted at length in nationalist tracts, and through his pages Hely Hutchinson's work was revived from a century of neglect. In 1881 Edward Blackburne quoted Hely Hutchinson extensively in a tract entitled *Causes of the decadence of the industries of Ireland*. An even more influential factor in the evolution of thought on Irish economic development was the reprinting in 1882 and again in 1888 of Hely Hutchinson's tract itself. The reprinting in 1882 was, according to the editor's introduction, inspired by 'the effort for the revival of our Native Industries' and was undertaken in the editor's words 'with the desire to contribute somewhat to the all-important and patriotic impulse'. In 1886, the year of the first home rule bill, appeared MacNeill Swift's *English interference with Irish industries*, based largely on quotations from Hely Hutchinson.

Hely Hutchinson's account is doubtful: it is not even representative of eighteenth-century writing. But the appeal of his thesis was strengthened by the fact that it was accepted by non-nationalists no less than nationalists. Indeed it was after all Froude, though out of sympathy with Irish nationalist aspiration, who had brought Hely Hutchinson to public attention again. In 1892 with the appearance of his great *History of Ireland in the eighteenth century* the weight of Lecky's authority confirmed the already general acceptance of Hely Hutchinson's views. The general interest in historical issues at this time was polemical. Such an interest does not of course thrive on failure. But after the Parnell split and the defeat of the second home rule bill in 1893, it was prevented from waning by the report in 1896 of the Financial Relations Commission which bore out the nationalist contention that Ireland had been overtaxed. Nor did the academic interest, as opposed to the polemical interest, in Irish economic history die out, for the discussion of fiscal matters stimulated by the Commission's report led to the appearance in 1903 of the first scholarly work in Irish economic history: Alice Murray's *History of the commercial and financial relations between England and Ireland from the Restoration*. Its success is denoted by its reprinting four years later. This book is of especial interest because, while it contradicted the nationalist contention by arguing that over-taxation was simply a consequence of the incidence of indirect taxation on low incomes and was experienced as much in rural England, it accepted without reservation the now-established version of eighteenth-century economic history. Appearing a decade later than Lecky's work, it reinforced further the general acceptance of what had been enounced originally in the eighteenth century as a polemical and somewhat unrepresentative view. Ample historical arguments, sanctioned even by the authority of independent scholarship, were now available for use in the Sinn Féin case for political and economic autonomy. It is significant that most of the general works on Irish economic history appeared at the peak of the political struggle between 1918 and 1921. The subsequent decline in interest was in keeping with the marked political motivation of study of the subject in the previous two hundred years.

A reason helping to explain the successful acceptance of this interpretation in the late nineteenth century was the growing importance of the land question as a political issue. Economic backwardness was attributed to the inequities of the land system, and the political prominence of the issue in the late nineteenth century led to its writing backwards into Irish history in the terms in which Irish nationalists and land leaguers wished to see it. Sigerson in 1871 had written a partisan *History of the land tenures and landed classes of Ireland*. Just over thirty years later, one of the main protagonists of the struggle, Michael Davitt, wrote *The fall of feudalism in Ireland*, seeing the land struggle as one of the main themes of Irish history in recent centuries. However, the outbreak of the land war at the end of the 1870's was as much a result of the rapid growth of national and democratic consciousness in very recent decades as of the depression of the late 1870's which was its occasion. Political hostility to the landlords inevitably was leading to the attribution to them of a role of political and economic oppression, a picture which became more clearly defined as political conflict sharpened. It is clear that contemporaries themselves had some difficulty in justifying this view. For instance, a witness before a parliamentary enquiry based his assertion about the harmful uncertainty that the system caused among tenants on the argument that one bad landlord in a locality destroyed confidence in all the rest. It is doubtful whether this assertion is true; but it does illustrate the rather special premises on which some assertions had to rely when closely questioned. However, given the growth of political hostility, a partisan account of preceding rural history was inevitable. Nor did historians in any way moderate the polemical presentation. In fact, they served to make the picture more unrealistic. Murray's work, for instance, distorted the picture of eighteenth-century rural history by wholesale acceptance of Newenham's thesis that pasture farming spread poverty through Ireland in the eighteenth century until the trend was reversed by the promotion of grain growing in the final two decades of the century. Newenham's work, written shortly after the Union, was an apologia for the economic policies of Grattan's Parliament and exaggerated the significance of its agricultural policy by an uncritical acceptance of previous expressions of fear about a decline in arable farming. In consequence his conclusions gave support to an unreliable picture of rural conditions.

Our knowledge of Irish economic history is based largely on premises selected during the political agitations of the late nineteenth century. A number of important qualifications must be made. First, the continuity of depression has been greatly exaggerated. There was no long-term depression in the eighteenth century. This was true of industry. It was the case also for agriculture. The late nineteenth-century land agitation created a vested interest in exaggerating the degree of continuity in the land question. There is little continuity or, outside the congested dis'ricts, even similarity between the rural poverty described in reports in the 1830's and 1840's and the unrest in the 1870's and 1880's. In the former case, poverty was marked among cottiers; in the latter case the catalysing forces were the economic depression of the late 1870's and the new political consciousness of farmers. Secondly, it is misleading to see rural Ireland as homogeneous. The distinction between cottier and farmer is essential in pre-famine history. It was indeed the extinction of the cottier and the decline in the number of farm labourers in post-Famine Ireland which simplified the social pattern of rural Ireland. Without such simplification the transfer of land ownership to the tenant would have failed to act as it did in the simplified social conditions of the late nineteenth century as an answer to agrarian unrest.

Nevertheless, even making allowances for overstatement, Ireland's underdevelopment in the nineteenth century is obvious. Industrial decline within the country and the contrast that advances elsewhere afforded both emphasised this. To a large extent this decline was inevitable; after mid-century decline was true less dramatically of rural England as well. There is of course no easy explanation of decline. Lack of capital was not a cause. It is doubtful also if the limitations of the educational system were responsible. The system was defective in England also. The lack of adequate native coal supplies contributed, but only to a limited extent. Coal was as cheap as in many parts of England outside the mining areas, and in Belfast it was little cheaper than elsewhere. Poor entrepreneurship may have been at fault, and the success of individual business and the industralisation of the north-east may confirm this. But it is not easy to determine whether this was a fundamental obstacle or itself in part a reflection of difficulties and declining population. It is far from clear whether there was any alternative to the course events took, or to what extent well-directed human resources or economic policies might have overcome the environment. Fiscal policy is relevant, but in the nineteenth century the advocacy of a fiscal policy by repealers was invariably a substitute for an economic policy rather than an economic policy in itself.

In the last analysis only two things stand out with certainty. First, Ireland was within the largely domestic technology of the eighteenth century a highly developed and rapidly expanding economy. Secondly, its proximity to the leader of the Industrial Revolution and the dramatic reductions in transport costs in the nineteenth century in conjunction left its small-scale and domestic industries vulnerable in a more fiercely competitive age. By comparison with many areas in Europe its striking contraction was in part at least the price it paid for its equally striking growth and expansion in the previous century. This of course conflicts with what became the orthodoxy of Irish economic history in the late 1870's and 1880's. But the orthodoxy that emerged at that time reflected the economic malaise of the period, and its acceptance was secured in the powerful upsurge of political feeling, which in time undermined both the land system and the Union

FURTHER READING

I

THE IRISH ECONOMY IN THE EIGHTEENTH CENTURY

L. M. Cullen, 'The value of contemporary printed sources for Irish economic history in the eighteenth century', *Irish Historical Studies*, vol. xiv, no. 54 (September, 1964)

L. M. Cullen, 'Problems in the interpretation and revision of eighteenth century Irish economic history', *Transactions of the Royal Historical Society*, 5th series, vol. xvii (1967)

Michael Drake, 'The Irish demographic crisis of 1740-41', *Historical Studies*, vol. vi, ed. T. W. Moody (London, 1968)

Irish Economic Documents, H. W. Stationery Office, Belfast, for the Public Record Office of Northern Ireland, 1967

II

THE RISE OF THE LINEN INDUSTRY

C. Gill, *The rise of the Irish linen industry* (Oxford, 1925, reprinted 1964)

J. Horner, *The linen trade of Europe during the spinning-wheel period* (Belfast, 1920)

E. R. R. Green, *The Lagan Valley, 1800-50 a local history of the industrial revolution* (London, 1949)

E. R. R. Green, *The industrial archaeology of county Down* (Belfast, 1963)

III

CATHOLICS IN ECONOMIC LIFE

M. Wall, 'The Catholics of the towns and the quarterage dispute', *Irish Historical Studies*, vol. viii, no. 30 (September, 1952)

M. Wall, 'The rise of a Catholic middle class in eighteenth-century Ireland, *Irish Historical Studies*, vol. xi, no. 42 (September, 1958)

M. Wall, 'The Catholic merchants, manufacturers and traders of

Dublin, 1778-1782', *Reportorium Novum: Dublin Diocesan Historical Record* vol. ii (1959-60)

John Brady, *Catholics and Catholicism in the eighteenth-century press* (Maynooth, 1965)

Robert E. Burns, 'The Catholic relief act in Ireland, 1778, *Church History*, vol. xxxii (1963)

IV
CAPITAL IN THE IRISH ECONOMY

F. G. Hall, *History of the Bank of Ireland* (Dublin and Oxford, 1949)

E. W. Henry and Louis J. Heelan, 'Capital in Irish industry', *Journal of the Statistical and Social Inquiry Society of Ireland*, vol xx (1962-3)

Joseph Lee, 'The provision of capital for early Irish railways', *Irish Historical Studies*, vol. xvi, no. 61 (March, 1968)

H. W. Robinson, *A history of accountants in Ireland* (Dublin, 1964)

V
POPULATION GROWTH AND THE IRISH ECONOMY

K. H. Connell, *The population of Ireland, 1750-1845* (Oxford, 1950)

Michael Drake, 'Marriage and population growth in Ireland, 1750-1845', *Economic History Review*, second series, vol. xvi, no. 2 (December, 1963)

Michael Drake, 'The Irish demographic crisis of 1740-41', *Historical Studies* vol. vi, ed. T. W. Moody (London, 1968)

Reports of the Commission on emigration and other population problems, 1948-54 (Dublin, n.d.)

VI
THE RAILWAYS IN THE IRISH ECONOMY

J. C. Conroy, *A history of railways in Ireland* (London, 1928)

V. T. H. and D. R. Delany, *The canals of the South of Ireland* (Newton Abbott, 1966), ch. IX

Joseph Lee, 'The construction costs of early Irish railways', *Business History* vol. ix (1967)

W. A. McCutcheon, 'Ulster railway engineering and architecture', *Ulster Journal of Archaeology*, third series, vol. xxvii (1964)

B. R. Mitchell, 'The coming of the railway and United Kingdom economic growth' *Journal of economic history*, vol. xxiv (1964)

K. A. Murray, *The Great Northern Railway (Ireland)* (Dublin, 1944)

VII
INDUSTRIAL DECLINE IN THE NINETEENTH CENTURY

P. Lynch and J. Vaizey, *Guinness's brewery in the Irish economy* (Cambridge, 1960)

G. O'Brien, *Economic history of Ireland from the Union to the Famine* (London, 1921)

W. P. Coyne (ed.), *Ireland, industrial and agricultural* (Dublin, 1902)

E. J. Riordan, *Modern Irish trade and industry* (London, 1920)

Select Committee on industries (Ireland), 1884-5, Parliamentary Papers.

VIII
THE INDUSTRIALISATION OF THE NORTH-EAST

J. C. Beckett, and R. E. Glasscock (ed), *Belfast, the origin and growth of an industrial city* (London, 1967)

C. Gill, *The rise of the Irish linen industry* (Oxford, 1925), reprinted 1964

E. R. R. Green, *The Lagan Valley, 1800-50, a local history of the industrial revolution* (London, 1949)

T. W. Moody, and J. C. Beckett (ed.), *Ulster since 1800, a political and economic survey* (London, 1954)

T. W. Moody, and J. C. Beckett (ed.), *Ulster since 1800, second series, a social survey* (London, 1957)

T. Wilson (ed.), *Ulster under home rule: a study of the political and economic problems of Northern Ireland* (London, 1955)

IX
IRISH ECONOMIC HISTORY: FACT AND MYTH

L. M. Cullen, *Life in Ireland* (London, 1968)

W. P. Coyne (ed.), *Ireland, industrial and agricultural* (Dublin, 1902)

A. E. Murray, *History of the commercial and financial relations between England and Ireland from the Restoration* (London, 1903)